POPULATION
POLLUTION and
PROPHECY

Leslie H. Woodson

Fleming H. Revell Company
Old Tappan, New Jersey

Unless otherwise identified, Scripture quotations in this volume are from the King James Version of the Bible.

Scripture quotations identified RSV are from the Revised Standard Version of the Bible, copyrighted 1946 and 1952.

Scripture references identified LB are from The Living Bible, copyright © 1971 Tyndale House Publishers, Wheaton, Illinois. Used by permission.

Scripture references identified ASV are from The American Standard Version of the Revised Bible, copyrighted 1946 by the International Council of Religious Education, and used by permission.

Library of Congress Cataloging in Publication Data

Woodson, Leslie H   , date
    Population, pollution, and prophecy.

  Bibliography: p.
  1. Bible-Prophecies.   I. Title.
BS647.2.W63   220.1'5   73–7967
ISBN 0–8007–0621–8

BY *Leslie H. Woodson*

Hell and Salvation
Population, Pollution, and Prophecy

Contents

Introduction

Nothing is more on the minds of modern men than the ominous threat of being squeezed out of the world or poisoned to death. Men of science are telling us that the terror of the bomb has been eclipsed by the growing fear of overpopulation and pollution. The human race has created a gigantic survival problem and it looks as if there is no known solution even to the experts. We have gotten ourselves into a king-size dilemma. While there is no lack of writing on these subjects from both a scientific and a moral stance, there seems to be little which relates the contemporary world's number one sociological problem to biblical prophecy.

This book could be called, *Three Ps In A Pod.* Population, pollution, and prophecy belong in the same household because of their close kinship with one another. The frightening future confronting the world today has resulted from man's exploitation of the Creator's good earth and his refusal to be responsible for his stewardship. In our determination to be gods, we are guilty of having ignored Him who made all things and seeks to redeem a fallen world. God knew that mankind would take this course and He also knew what the consummation would be. For this reason it is wise to search His Word if population and pollution, as well as all other sin-rooted scourges, are to be seen in proper focus.

As would be expected, this work is more concerned with the answer than with the question. Although the customary approach today is to dwell on our problems and magnify the questions without offering much in the way of solutions, the following approach will be vastly different. What the world wants is an answer! There is no scarcity of questions. The problem will be succinctly stated in the first two chapters and the rest of the book will be an engagement with the Scriptures and the light which they throw on the subject. If an answer is to be found, it will have to be discovered in the biblical record of history and prophecy.

The Bible is God's answer book. Within its contents is found the key to the past, present, and future. It is not the will of our heavenly Father to keep His children in the dark. Those who dwell in the dark have never experienced the divine light which dispels the fear that grows out of uncertainty. God's written Word is not a mysterious collection of mystical literature. It is the *revealed* Word given by the inspiration of the Holy Spirit to men chosen by God to serve as channels for divine communication. It is the will of God that we know His plan of the ages, its stages of progression, and its consummation. Naturally, we cannot know that plan if we do not study it. It is the careful study of the Lord's design for the solution to the world's ills that we are attempting to pursue in these pages. Our prayer is that the Holy Spirit, who guides us into all truth, will enlighten our minds and warm our hearts as we see the eternal plan unfold in the word of prophecy.

LESLIE H. WOODSON

1
Our Population Dilemma

A Divine Order Carried Out

At the dawn of human creation God ordered Adam and Eve to "multiply and replenish the earth" (Genesis 1:28). This was the Creator's way of insuring the continuance of what He had begun, a kind of built-in perpetual momentum for human existence. Man was to be repetitive on his own. It was to be a chain reaction by which, once started on the earth, the human species would be permanently and perennially renewed.

Only once did God interrupt the natural mushrooming process of human life. That was when the world became so corrupt that the earth had to be cleansed by a flood of waters which destroyed all but eight persons. When the waters subsided and Noah came forth from the ark into a world emptied of human life, God again repeated the order which He had given to Adam: ". . . Be fruitful, and multiply, and replenish the earth" (Genesis 9:1). The plan had not changed since the beginning. God's will was that the man, created in the divine likeness, should reproduce in kind until the whole earth was seeded with human life.

No one knows how old the earth is or precisely how long ago man appeared on the scene. Abraham lived about four thousand years ago at a time when the world seems to have been rather sparsely settled. Less than fifty million people may have inhabited the entire earth in his day. Since the period from Adam to Abraham is not known to us we have no way of determining what the rate of growth may have been on a time schedule.

In the days of Christ there were approximately two hundred million people in the world. By the time of the seventeenth-century Puritans, the population figure had climbed to a half-billion. Within the next two centuries the world's human family increased to one billion for the first time in history. Today there are nearly four billion people inhabiting the earth and scientists predict as many as seven billion by the year 2000, an approximate doubling of our present population. (For a sobering study of population explosion see Paul R. Ehrlich's *The Population Bomb.*)

Any projection of population growth is dependent on many variables which cannot be known with any degree of accuracy. Ehrlich, professor of biology at Stanford University, cites the low, median, and high variants as well as the "constant fertility, no migration" estimate. The extremes for world population in the year 2000 are 5,448,533,000 as against 7,522,218,000. An approximate average would be six and one-half billion. (From *Population, Resources, Environment* by Paul R. and Anne H. Ehrlich, pages 336-340.)

It is easy to see that the rate of reproduction has accelerated with the passing millennia. The span of time required for the population to double itself has grown shorter and shorter. While the total doubled only once during the period from Alexander the Great to the great Mohammed (approximately one thousand years), today's population doubles twice in an average man's lifetime. At this rate it will not be long until there is STANDING ROOM ONLY on the earth.

Of all the divine commands given to man (many of which he has broken and refused to obey), the order to "multiply and replenish the earth" has been carried out to perfection. The fact of the matter is that we have *overdone* it! This is not to imply that God has been caught off guard by the excess numbers of people now in existence or the frightening prospects of further population growth. The Creator must have known that our present state of affairs would finally develop. And it is the opinion of the author of this book that He has planned for just such an emergency.

Simply a Matter of Mathematics

An old, oft-used, and unbelievable trick is to ask a fresh recruit in the world of riddles which he would prefer—to work for a month at one hundred dollars per day or to work the same number of days at a penny for the first day, twice a penny the second day, and double the sum each day thereafter. Invariably, the would-be-laborer will impulsively choose one hundred dollars per day. It only takes a fleeting second to ring up a mental total of three thousand dollars for the month. That is a lot of money in anyone's language.

To ascertain the wages for thirty days at a penny doubled each day is considerably more difficult. At once, however, it is assumed that the total would be far less than three thousand dollars. When the facts are in, this assumption is proved incorrect. Working by this plan thirty days labor pays $10,737,418.23. And if the month has thirty-one days in it, this figure becomes over twenty-one million dollars!

By this simple arithmetic one can readily see how the world's population has exploded so suddenly in our time. And if the trend continues unabated we may expect more serious problems—far more serious. Should the world still be around one hundred years from now there will be twenty-eight billion people. In two hundred years there will be two hundred twenty-four billion. And in three hundred years the staggering figure will be nearly one trillion people. As if this were not incredible enough, the period of time necessary to double the population will decrease as rapidly as the population figure increases. On this basis the number of people for each of the above dates would be even larger than we have projected.

Little reason exists for becoming too upset about what may happen a century from now. Most scientists believe that the big population bomb will go off around the end of this century. Between 35 and 40 percent of the world's people are still in their mid-teens. By A.D. 2,000, or before, we will see the biggest crop of newborn children in the history of the human race. Our problems have just begun!

The Reason for Our Distress

In addition to the natural effects of doubling the population in shorter intervals, medical science has done a phenomenal job in conquering disease. Most of the scourges which once took the lives of multitudes have been attacked and defeated. Technologists have produced a maze of mechanical equipment which diagnose and treat both physical and mental maladies. There is nothing unusual about an ingeniously invented device absolutely taking over completely when the human body stops functioning. Iron lungs have been in use for a number of years and now we have pacemakers which can be surgically placed within the body to force the heart to beat and to control its regularity. When the kidneys cease to operate, the patient can be put on a machine which literally washes the poison from the blood and restores it clean to the body.

Little can happen to the modern man for which some corrective mechanical device is not readily available. This is true from the most minor illnesses to the major problems. More people are living longer because of the technological inventions of the scientific laboratories. Of late we are hearing more and more talk about freezing the human body under continued surveillance until a remedy is found for its disease. At that time it is assumed that the body can be thawed and returned to new life. All this is still in the beginning stages, but in light of the astounding things already happening, no one dares to suggest that such an eerie dream may not become a reality.

Miracle drugs are responsible for saving multiplied thousands of lives each year—people who would have died in earlier times from the same ailments. The infant mortality rate has been greatly decreased and man's life-span is being stretched out by new and better methods of treatment. Some scientists are even talking about physical immortality by which man may exist indefinitely by transplants. As parts of the body wear out or become defective, spare parts stored in a transplant bank can be surgically exchanged. This includes not only internal organs such as hearts, kidneys, livers, stomachs, and brains, but external faculties such as arms, legs, and reproductive organs as well. It is even suggested that eventually entire heads, not just the brain, will be transplanted. While one must react to such proposals for earthly immortality, it has to be admitted that the effort to achieve such a questionable boon might contribute to the projected population problems.

With more people being born each year and the longevity of the human species being extended at the same time, it can be readily observed that our situation is bound to get worse. The human race is stretching itself at both ends rather than in the middle. Thus, in the foreseeable future it is reasonable to assume that the numbers of children and youth (at one end of the age scale) and senior citizens (at the other end) will outdistance those of reproductive and middle years. Our generation gap is of no significance now in comparison to what it would be under conditions like those we have here projected for the future.

An Approach Toward Solution

All the knowledge of several branches of science is being combined to find a solution to the enormous problem of overpopulation. Few reputable scientists actually have much confidence that any of the proposed remedies will work. It is doubtful that enough people would cooperate with any suggested solution to make much difference. This is so for at least two reasons. Most of us do not fully grasp the gravity of the situation. We cannot really believe that possibilities could be as bad as we have heard. Furthermore, even those who have some understanding of the overall problem do not have consciences strong enough to encourage needed action. Most of us convince ourselves that what we ourselves do cannot make much difference since no one else is apt to do anything either.

The one approach thus far tried seriously is that of planned parenthood. Tons of literature have been written on the subject, government clinics have been established for instruction, churches and schools continue to contribute their influence, and free medical and mechanical aids are being provided for those too impoverished to pay for methods of control. Families are being urged to limit their children to two as a sensible way to slow down population growth. It is pointed out that, in many instances, children would be better cared for in smaller family units. This would be a fringe benefit in addition to stunting the population growth. Some married people have sought to fit into the new plan for smaller families, but the problem remains far from solved.

Contraceptives are now available in varied forms and almost anyone can get them regardless of age or circumstances. They can be worn, inserted, or taken internallly. Surgery is often used to render a mother incapable of bearing children and men are now undergoing a minor surgery known as *vasectomy* which results in sterility. All of this is a part of our present approach to finding a practical and workable solution to the monstrous problem of too many people.

Weaknesses in the Approach

In addition to the fact that most people are not paying much attention to the scare tactics of an alarmed scientific community, there are some disappointing developments in the whole plan. Easy access to contraceptives has encouraged untold millions of young people to engage in sexual intercourse who would have been afraid to do so without the modern security of the Pill. Unwanted and unexpected pregnancies have often resulted because of too much dependence on the promise of medical science.

As would be expected, the wide use of the Pill has carried with it a changed attitude on the sacredness of life. Abortion laws are being relaxed in the wake of a flood of so-called unplanned babies. Some estimates suggest that as many as one-third of the babies born to first-time mothers are conceived outside the institution of marriage. This is a reflection on our changing views on the sacredness of human life. Though the birthrate has decreased slightly in general, the number of illegitimate births is on the increase. What we may be doing in cutting down the size of families is actually encouraging the birth of children to contraceptive-saturated single women. The whole institution of marriage may die and the race revert to existing and breeding like animals in the field.

With abortion available under the law for nearly any reason, we may expect to see our hospitals, clinics, and doctors' offices filled with women standing in line to be miscarried. More and more the decision is being left to the mother—if she happens to have an understanding doctor. Even if this should eliminate a few hundred thousand babies a year it will make no noticeable dent in the expanding population. And the emotional damage done to the mother—not to mention the growing disrespect for human life—might be far worse ultimately than permitting the fetus the right to live.

A Projected Control Possibility

Debate has raged for years over whether a government, in order to control its population or balance its welfare budget, has the right to enforce a limit on the size of one's family. Under the existing welfare program it seems almost profitable for the indigent to have another child each year. Each dependent child increases the support received. Therefore, as a rule, our largest families are to be found in the slums or among the extremely poor.

To pass legislation which would limit these and other families as to the number of children permitted would require either a police state or mass sterilization. Cutting down the welfare payment might help but it would not get to the heart of the matter. One can imagine what it would be like to live in a police state where everyone is constantly checked to see whether new members have been secretly added to the family! The fear of living under that kind of brutality which would possibly destroy either the new child or the parent responsible is not hard to understand.

Enforced sterility seems to be a more humane method. Such a move may become a necessity in underdeveloped nations where starvation is a constant way of life. It may also become the only answer to our burgeoning welfare program. Certainly it is better not to bring a child into the world than to give him birth without reasonable chance of survival. Yet, none of us can allow himself to think about this kind of procedure for very long without facing the grim possibility that some of the world's greatest men were born in extreme poverty. Under such a proposed plan they would have been denied the right to be.

Aside from this haunting fact is the whole matter of ethics. Does a nation have the right to interfere in this most private and personal area of a man's life? Are we engaged in a moral crime to treat people as though they were barnyard cattle emasculated at the will of others? Who would make the decision as to the size of families and what would be done with persons who managed to evade the law and "criminally" produce more children than permitted? And what would happen to mothers who were sterilized after having the allotted number of children in the tragic event her offspring died? The ethics involved in designing such a control measure cannot be overlooked.

Space Colonies as a Last Resort

Oceanologists are talking not only of living off the nutrients available from cultivating the seas but of living in the oceans themselves. If man could devise some inexpensive method of creating cities under water he would help the immediate population squeeze. Unquestionably, scientists can do this for a few hundred men in a manned undersea station. But to think of millions of people dwelling in similar circumstances is practically impossible from both sociological and economical perspectives. And if we should admit that miracles of science still happen, what will we do when the oceans are full?

That brings us to one of the most recent scientific proposals. Seriously projected as a possibility is the colonization of distant planets. Our worldwide space program has been geared to exploring the moon to see whether human life could survive there. Billions of dollars have been invested in this exciting spectacular. Now it is known that men from the earth could not exist on the moon because there is no oxygen there. Furthermore, scientists are equally certain that the atmosphere on Mars and Venus is just as unacceptable to human life as we know it. Thus, the colonizing of these near planets is out of the question. Even if we could get enough people transported there to ease the pressure on earth, they could not survive without artificially controlled environment.

Perhaps there is a more distant planet or star where the environment would be more conducive to man's survival. Should we travel to the nearest star at the speed of light the round trip would take nearly ten years. (The nearest star is 4.3 light years away. A light year is 5.88 million million miles. Light travels at a speed of 186,000 miles per second. The round trip would be 50,568,000,000,000 miles which, at uninterrupted travel, would take eight and one-half years.)

But consider what these voyages would entail. How big could we build such rocket ships? How many people would they carry? How much would they cost and how many of them would be needed to get ahead of the population explosion? The plan to colonize outer space with earth people may be a good idea but it has no chance of working. Apparently, God intended for us to stay right here! To continue to dream of living somewhere other than on this planet is to dwell in a world of gossamer wings with Peter Pan.

Humanity's Dead End

In light of the emerging dilemma of having just too many people on the earth, what can be done? Are there any measures known to man which can offer some ray of hope? If *everyone* would cooperate with the proposal to plan smaller families there might be a chance. We are completely unrealistic to think that everyone—or even the majority of the world's people—will cooperate with anything suggested either by the governments of the world or the churches in it. Neither political persuasion nor ecclesiastical ethics have much influence on a race of people trained in permissiveness and bent on self-rule. And without the full cooperation of the men and women who create the problem there can be no known solution.

Multitudes poke their heads in the sand and refuse to see the clamoring masses on tomorrow's horizon. Just as many have decided that the whole thing is hopeless anyway (if the bomb does not get us the pollution will), so what is the use in worrying about population? More rational people are deeply concerned—some are even frightened for their grandchildren who will have to live in an overcrowded and impossible world. They are unwilling to cop out and let humanity go down the drain.

Men come up with newer and better ideas every day which appear to hold some possible answers. So far these human ideas only add to the complex confusion. Man is unequal to the task of saving his world. An example of the dilemma may be seen in the tug between the human ethic and the human reason. While we have managed to greatly reduce the infant mortality rate, we are now deciding in favor of abortions to solve the overpopulation problem by doing what nature did before we got so smart. Obviously, abortions are also being endorsed for the sake of the pregnant mother herself, but the fear of population explosion gets involved, too.

And while we have prolonged man's life to the point where some scientists are predicting that persons born in 1973 have a good chance of living to be one hundred fifty years old—at the same time we are debating the right and wrong of euthanasia. Is it possible that we have interfered too much with nature's simple remedies for overpopulation?

Added to the confusion is the fact that—though man has always considered war to be ethically wrong—never in history has there been such a worldwide denouncement of military combat. If the masses ever rule out war (which has been one method of controlling the population in the past), what will this mean for the future? Let no one consider this as an endorsement of war anymore than we are endorsing an increased mortality rate for infants! We are only looking at facts as they now exist. It is not difficult to see that everything we do complicates the whole problem until man is at last beginning to admit that he is at a dead end and no further maneuvering will help. Even scientists are now talking freely about the inevitable end of the world—and that could happen by any one of several grim catastrophes. In the next chapter we shall look at some of the sticky issues which cling like glue to the basic population dilemma.

2
Related Problems

A General Picture

As the number of people increases, more and more of earth's natural resources are exhausted. These resources may finally be depleted entirely because man will use them faster than the earth can reproduce them. But there is more to it than this: As these resources are used they are not actually destroyed. They change form and are dumped back on the earth, in the water, or in the air. This means that more people using more resources produce more pollutants.

Ecologists are crying out in despair against what man is doing to his environment. It is evident that the world and the atmosphere around it are being turned into a giant dump heap. At the rate we are going, the human race may someday be like loathsome vermin crawling in a dunghill. And only if we develop different lungs and kidneys will we be able to breathe the air and drink the water. Everything is becoming contaminated.

It can readily be seen that population and pollution are related one to the other. If we can reduce the expected population growth we will automatically reduce some of the areas of pollution. On the other hand, unless something is done soon about pollutants, the entire human family may be obliterated. That is an awesome thought but it is nonetheless true. It is not a matter of deciding which needs to be worked on first since both threats are closely interrelated. Both must be confronted at the same time, and something must be done at once. Perhaps it is worse than that. From a purely selfish concern there may be little time to lose.

There are those who will insist that these remarks are too pessimistic. It depends on what one is looking for. Others may feel that they are too optimistic in that they suggest a *chance* for survival. Prevention of pollution saturation is destined to be at the top of the list of priorities in the effort to survive at all. The dedicated work of every world citizen must be brought into play if the suicidal trend is ever to be reversed.

Air We Cannot Afford to Breathe

It is a reasonable assumption that—within a few years—men will be able to live only in cities covered by huge domes under which the air is regularly purified. In order to go outside one would be forced to wear a mask equipped with capsuled oxygen. Such excursions into the outside world would be discouraged except in extreme necessity. The risk would be too great even with a mask since the air might be so polluted as to be irritating to the flesh itself.

The smog over Los Angeles today is like pure oxygen compared to what can be expected in the next quarter of a century. And it will not be confined to particular areas but will encase the whole globe like a wet, oppressive blanket. Settling on the world like fallout from a nuclear explosion are enormous quantities of smoke, ash, sulphur, dust, and numerous chemically-destructive gases. This is already the case and it gets worse every year. Soon the saturation point will be reached and the human race will be doomed.

As nuclear activity is accelerated, we will have magnified amounts of pollutants. A step-up in nuclear-powered machinery is all but inevitable. Future cars may have nuclear engines though the move at present seems to be in the direction of electric cars. Even electric cars, however, could be dependent on nuclear energizing. Such energy may be harnessed in the operation of huge factories for production of both heat and power. The radioactive pollutants given off by the use of this method would be devastating to plant life as well as to the human animal and his cousins in the fields.

Respiratory ailments are on the rise. Emphysema is swiftly challenging other modern diseases for number-one spot on the list of human killers. Lung cancer threatens more men and women every day. No longer is it enough to discontinue smoking as protection against lung cancer. Just breathing the industrial, commercial, chemical-laden air seems to be enough to adversely affect even nonsmokers.

Continued dumping of our wastes into the air will ultimately so clog the biosphere that the rays of the sun will heat the particles so intensely as to raise the earth's temperature. A few degrees difference could be disastrous. With increased heat, the ice at the polar caps would melt and raise the level of our oceans enough to flood much of the land area. And with the population figures soaring, the last thing we can afford to lose is a single acre of ground! All this is directly related: more people, more technology, more pollution.

Water We Cannot Afford to Drink

Lately we have been bombarded by warnings related to water contamination. From small townships to metropolitan industrial centers our streams, rivers, lakes, and oceans are being filled with noxious waste. By the end of this century, every major source of water will be so polluted as to be useless unless the contamination is curbed. Even in towns without factories, the water has a bad odor and taste because of the excessive amounts of chemical additives necessary to make it safe to drink. Obviously, the chemicals themselves are damaging our own body systems. Again we are "caught between a rock and a hard place."

The world's seas are filled with plant life called *phytoplankton* which produces and sustains about 65 percent of the oxygen in our atmosphere. Because of pollutants, this plant life is being destroyed in great quantities. Yet, we continue to dump human and industrial refuse into the oceans as man shuts his eyes to the death he is creating for himself and his children. The fact that fish in our seas are often so filled with chemical wastes that they are unfit to eat is a commentary on the plight we are describing.

Since the beginning of creation not one drop of water has been added or subtracted from the original supply. It changes forms and is used over and over again but eventually it returns to the seas where the cycle is repeated. Salt from gradually-rising water tables is now being found in underground fresh-water channels. If the ice caps should melt (as mentioned above), the salt from the seas would render much of the land untillable—land not covered by ocean water but still recipient of salt seepage. If we could stop the pollution of our water systems and control the contaminants in the air, we still have to solve the problem of where to get the water needed for twice our present population in the year 2000. Scientists have no idea where all this water can be found!

If a new source of water is discovered (possibly desalting ocean water), it will still be urgent that some quick remedy be found for the pollution spilled into it by our proliferating technological society and by a 100 percent increase in the number of people using it. Thus we not only have an air pollution problem, but also the puzzling riddle of contaminated water. Our backs are against the wall.

Land We Cannot Use

According to some experts, at least two acres of productive land are needed to provide the minimal diet requirements for one man's basic health needs. A comparison of the number of acres of tillable soil now available with the number of people living in the world indicates that this ratio is not obtainable now. If the population increases at the rate predicted, the number of acres of productive soil available per person will be eleven billion short.

As if this were not enough of a problem to haunt us, vast stretches of this usable soil are being carelessly neglected, desecrated, and covered with defiling refuse. Manifestly, our garbage has to be placed somewhere. If it is not dumped in the seas then it must be dumped on the earth. There is nowhere else to put it. Of course, it has been suggested that giant spaceships could transfer our garbage into the heavens beyond the pull of gravity. This would load space beyond our earth with even more particles to be heated by the sun and thus raise the world's temperature. Such earth fever would be disastrous for human life. A variation on this proposal: Garbage could be rocketed toward the sun where both the carrier and its rotting cargo would be incinerated. The cost of such a sanitation service in itself would be enough to discourage use of this plan.

We already have arrived at the point where it is not easy to find additional land area which is needed for burying the dead. Mausoleums provide one way of using less space. It has been suggested that bodies could be buried in stacks or interred upright. Cremation appears to be a good way to conserve land area, but a massive program of cremation would add more pollutants to the atmosphere! There is no simple answer. Maybe there is no answer at all!

Animal life and plant growth are both having a rough time in this maze. Pesticides and chemical treatment of plants have proved injurious to the animals that need the plants for food. In turn, people who eat these animals are also harmed. Artificial foods are being made to fill the gap created by this problem. Eventually we may have to face illnesses resulting from too much food manufactured with synthetic nutrients.

Starvation for the Future

Over three and one half million men, women, and children die of starvation each year, according to Salem Kirban in *Guide to Survival* (page 56). That is a staggering figure. To put it another way, over four hundred people starve to death every hour. Kirban also states that a family of seven people die from starvation every second. In America we are hard pressed to grasp the horror of this fact because ours is a land of plenty where masses of starving people in the streets are not seen. Nevertheless, in many countries of the world it is an almost impossible task to bury the bodies as fast as they fall. And no one in his right mind can doubt that such conditions may someday prevail right here in the land of Western luxury.

With our soil being depleted of its natural growth qualities and poisoned by our contaminants, it cannot be expected to produce enough for as many human beings as are anticipated within the next few years. As food becomes less plentiful, it will be priced higher until it is out of reach of all but a select group of wealthy citizens. Every inch of space in one's yard (and there will be no yards left soon in the press of people!) will be cultivated carefully to eke out a bare subsistence. Looking at these prospects makes the words of Jesus come alive: ". . . there will be famines . . . in various places: all this is but the beginning of the sufferings" (Matthew 24:7, 8 RSV). The days of which He spoke are here and the sane man knows that they are bound to get worse.

The earth absolutely cannot produce enough food for 6.5 billion people. If we are seriously counting on cultivating the sea for foodstuff we are not being very realistic. With the growing mortality rate of sea life there is little chance of much help there. Starvation is right in the middle of our radar screen and the human race is precisely on course.

Someone will immediately reply that such a deplorable situation will control the population explosion. To be sure, increased starvation will cut down the numbers of people in the world, but the human family will be "lucky" enough to utilize its technological skills so that the number of deaths will never equal the number of births. This will be done for a while by artificial foods even if they are nothing more than nutrient-saturated energy pills. It may be that enforced dieting will become the order of the day. Food will be rationed under carefully supervised governmental control. And all this will finally result in a dictator for the whole world who will demand that his identifying mark be branded on every forehead before one can buy food at all (Revelation 13:17). Undoubtedly, some form of tranquilizer will also be administered to people to numb them to reality and curb hunger riots. Population and starvation are closely intertwined, but it is prophetically clear that the latter —terrible as it will become—will not *solve* anything.

No Human Answer

Caught up in this melee of insurmountable obstacles to any kind of satisfying life in the future, man is apt to despair and lose hope. There is nothing man can do to solve the riddle of overpopulation. There is no *human* answer. Only those who are either too obtuse to see what is happening or those who are too obsessed with their own self-sufficiency can possibly continue to trust any man or group of men to save the world. A few decades ago the old liberals were sure that—given enough culture and education—the world would get better and better. They have been proved wrong—dead wrong. With all the refinements of modern education and philosophy the picture gets blacker. *Man* can provide no escape from the frightening prospects which lie ahead.

Let no one think that there is no way out of this alarming mess (as though it cannot be done unless man does it). Our whole problem stems from our neglect of God's will and disregard for His prophetic plan. The masses have never had time to read His Word and study it seriously. Perhaps it has not been so much a matter of lacking time as lacking the disposition to open oneself to divine truth. Whatever the reason may have been, there is appalling ignorance of the heart of the Bible and terrible fear for that very reason. There is an answer but it is not of man's making. It is God's answer and it is becoming clearer every day. The rest of this book will be dedicated to finding out just what that divine solution to overpopulation really is. We are about to embark on an awesome look at the future as God has planned it.

3
The Lift-Off

The Countdown Begins

Excitement is in the air. Men in white are scurrying about in a last-minute effort to get everything ready for blast-off. Specialists are poring over their intricate instruments, checking and rechecking every detail to be sure that nothing fails to function in the electronic devices so important to a space flight. Tracking stations have been set up all across the world to check the trajectory of the rocket-powered module. Mechanics specially trained for the job are busily engaged in fueling operations and last-minute adjustments. A lazy vapor seeps from the side of the mighty rocket squatting on its base like a wild beast ready to attack without warning.

Three men outfitted in luminous, balloonlike suits reminiscent of a Buck Rogers movie take an elevator to the capsule. Over their heads are glass bubbles which make them look like imaginary creatures from another planet. They look peculiar and walk in a strange kind of mechanical manner. These men have been training for months—perhaps years—for this moment. The discipline through which they have put themselves is incredible. And they have committed themselves to an austere way of living because they believe in what is going to happen. They are a part of a plan which is much bigger than any of them as individuals. No doubts linger in their minds. Though no one has ever been to the moon before, there is not the slightest lack of confidence that it is going to take place.

Masses of people are skeptical. Talk of going to the moon has been heard here and there for years. Some actually think it is about to transpire—but not everyone. Three strange-acting men will probably be killed in some kind of fiery blast before it is over. The whole idea is so idiotic. Why can men not stay here on earth where they belong? Why does anyone want to go flying off into some unknown world only to get blown up? It will never happen. Yet, the silly countdown continues: "*T* minus twenty-two minutes and counting. . . ." It would be a laughing matter if it were not that somebody is going to be killed in the wreckage. The whole scheme will make the United States the laughingstock of the whole world. Mumbling and shaking their heads at the stupidity being seen portrayed on their television screen, they retire to the kitchen for a snack. It is all so ridiculous.

"*T* minus three minutes and four seconds and counting. . . ." They rush back to the screen still shaking their heads in unbelief. "Four— three—two—one—ignition!" An explosion of orange fire rolls from beneath the rocket and slowly the big bird begins to rise from its nest. In a matter of seconds it is picking up speed and in only a few more it is out of sight. Technicians report all systems are working and the rocket is on course. Within a few minutes it is reported that the ship has passed the first danger point. Soon the first stage is completed on time, second stage on target, and the mission looks like a success. A few days later the astronauts are on the moon. Believe it or not, it had happened. What had been predicted was now history and those who did not believe could not accept what had taken place.

Another Countdown Has Begun

Excitement is in the air. But it is not at Cape Kennedy. It is all over the world. There is an air of expectancy among certain people. To be sure, not everyone is excited since many are so caught up with the awesome problems of a crumbling launching pad that they have forgotten or ignored the possibility of a launch altogether. For a long time this day has been planned. Men and women, young people and children, in invisible white garments are scurrying about to be sure that everything is ready. Specialists in prophecy are checking every detail and the trajectory is being studied carefully. Numbers of workers are set to the task of fueling and making the adjustments through prayer and witnessing.

The difference between this launch and the one at the Cape is that everybody involved in the preparation is going—not just three astronauts. Those engaged in getting themselves ready and recruiting others for the journey into space are thought to be a little odd. They have a stance which reminds one of the strange look and walk of the balloon-suited men in the moon capsule. But these people are a part of a plan, a *divine* plan, which they are as certain will be completed as were those dedicated astronauts confident of their flight to the moon.

There has been talk occasionally across the years about this religious notion of a flight into the heavens with Christ, but not many have paid any attention to it. It all seemed a little hairbrained to say the least. It is true that some people were preparing 'way back in the first century but it did not happen. The countdown has been going on for two thousand years. Some think that there have been times when God has interrupted the countdown with "*T* minus thirteen hundred years and holding . . ." or "*T* minus four hundred fifty years and holding. . . ," but most Christians believe that the counting has continued since the Ascension of Christ.

For two thousand years men and women have been training, disciplining themselves while the masses laughed them to scorn. To the man of the world—whether he is in the organized church makes little difference —the preparation which persons in the true Church are making for lift-off is a laughing matter. He will not even listen to what is being said. He is a non-Bible bigot who refuses to hear anything which he has decided is unacceptable to a sophisticated being on the pure basis of human logic alone. And so the world goes about its reckless way, disregarding all the signs that point to blast-off time. Yet, the countdown continues and the voice of Deity Control is saying, "*T* minus thirty years and counting . . . *T* minus twenty years and counting . . . *T* minus fifteen years and counting. . . ." No one knows for sure when the last seconds will tick away: "Four—three—two—one—ignition!"

The Whole World as a Launching Pad

In the moon shot a predetermined location on the earth's surface was chosen for the launch. Only from one spot could the astronauts be catapulted into their orbit around the moon. The chosen place was a restricted area at the edge of the Atlantic Ocean. Persons outside the grounds of Cape Kennedy were able to share in the historical lift-off only by watching from afar. Even men who were closely associated with the lunar program and actually on the grounds were not permitted to ride in the nose of the rocket. Three men out of all the world's billions were to experience the mighty surge of power which sent one lone spaceship into the starry heavens.

The launch which is scheduled to soon take place is not set for some restricted place on the world's surface. When the lift-off comes it will happen all over the earth at one and the same time. Neither space nor time constitutes a serious problem for Him who created both. The Eternal Spirit is always present in every place. And when He decides to overrule the forces of gravity which keep man on the earth, even graves will be broken apart and emptied of their tenants. So irresistible is the drawing power of the Lord that men and women of like nature, both dead and alive, will be magnetically pulled to Him. Millions of people from all over the world, people who have committed their lives in faith to the redeeming Christ, will join the One who saved them in the clouds of heaven. Nowhere in the Scriptures is this more vividly described than in the letter of Paul written to the church at Thessalonica.

For this we declare to you by the word of the Lord, that we who are alive, who are left until the coming of the Lord, shall not precede those who have fallen asleep. For the Lord himself will descend from heaven with a cry of command, with the archangel's call, and with the sound of the trumpet of God. And the dead in Christ will rise first; then we which are alive, who are left, shall be caught up together with them in the clouds to meet the Lord in the air; and so we shall always be with the Lord.

1 Thessalonians 4:15–17 RSV

When the Saviour was here in the flesh He employed this divine drawing power in a most unique manner on one particular occasion. It was a kind of prelude to that final day when He will "descend from heaven with a cry of command." Arriving at the home of Mary and Martha after their brother Lazarus had been dead for four days, Jesus had the stone removed from the tomb. Then, with a loud "cry of command," He called the name of him who was interred there and ordered that he come forth. At once the man arose, was stripped of his grave clothing, and enjoyed the fellowship of his Lord (John 11:1–44). Someday *every* grave which shelters the body of Christ's disciple will break open at that "cry of command." Had Jesus not called Lazarus by name that day in Bethany the entire cemetery would have been emptied! And when He comes with that divine shout from the clouds every redeemed man, woman, boy, and girl will hear his name in that cry and will rise to meet the Lord.

There will be apostles whose bodies have lain in some unknown grave since the first century, unsung heroes of the faith from across the centuries, and martyrs from many lands in that great crowd of the redeemed. Not one will be forgotten by God. Black Christians from the heart of Africa will be there. Brown-skinned followers of the Christ will join them from India, Spain, Mexico, and South America. Europeans, Orientals, Asiatics, Scandinavians, Polynesians, Australians, North Americans, and islanders from all over the earth will converge at that meeting in the air. The aged will be there and the children. Every period in Christian history is to be represented. From every quarter of the earth the people of the Lord shall come pouring in to be together forever. At last the Church for which He prayed will be one (John 17:23).

Some Will Not Have to Die

Since the beginning of time all men have shared the lot common to humanity. With the exception of Enoch and Elijah, every man born from Adam until the present time has been destined to die. It is true that those who die in the Lord will rise again when Christ returns. This is what Jesus was talking about when He said to Martha, ". . . I am the resurrection and the life; he who believes in me, though he die, yet shall he live, and whoever lives and believes in me shall never die . . ." (John 11:25, 26 RSV). In this word about *never* dying the Lord has reference to spiritual death which has no power over the Christian believer. But there are some people who will have the distinct privilege of never dying at all—spiritually or physically. These are the redeemed of the Lord who are still alive at the coming of Jesus the second time.

Being as human as the rest of us in his desire to meet the Saviour without the need of physical death, the Apostle Paul hoped that the Lord would come again in his own lifetime. In fact, he felt strongly about such a possibility. And that is the only correct attitude for Christians in every age. In his anxiousness for the *parousia* (the Greek New Testament word for *Second Coming* which we will use in this book), Paul excitedly explained to the members of the little church in Corinth:

> Lo! I tell you a mystery. We shall not all sleep, but we shall all be changed, in a moment, in the twinkling of an eye, at the last trumpet. For the trumpet will sound, and the dead will be raised imperishable, and we shall be changed.
>
> 1 Corinthians 15:51, 52 RSV

The *trumpet sound* to which he refers is the same as that mentioned in the earlier reference from the epistle to the Thessalonians. The "cry of command" and "the sound of the trumpet of God" will usher in "the resurrection of the just" (Luke 14:13). But it will also be the divine signal for a glorious change in those who are alive when the sound is heard. The apostle calls this change "a mystery." We cannot imagine how God will effect this metamorphosis, but there is no question about the certainty of its happening. It will happen "in a moment, in the twinkling of an eye." What God will do for His people at that time will be sudden and complete. There is no hint of an evolutionary change. The transformation will be as instantaneous as the change which comes to a hard grain of corn held over the fire until it pops into a fresh, white form.

No other explanation is given about the kind of change we may anticipate than Paul's statement about that which is perishable becoming imperishable and that which is mortal becoming immortal (1 Corinthians 15:42–44, 53). Apparently the transformation depicted here is the same as that hinted by John when he writes, ". . . we are God's children now; it does not yet appear what we shall be, but we know that when he appears we shall be like him for we shall see him as he is" (1 John 3:2 RSV). The change which materializes in that split moment of time will completely prepare the living believers for life in a brand-new dimension of existence. Whatever needs altering will be altered and made new even as the resurrected bodies of the dead believers. "We await a Saviour, the Lord Jesus Christ, who will change our lowly body to be like his glorious body, by the power which enables him even to subject all things to himself" (Philippians 3:20, 21 RSV).

When Jesus predicts those things to be looked for immediately prior to the Second Advent of the Son of God, He emphatically affirms with an *amen* to preface His divine Word, "Truly, I say to you, this generation will not pass away till all has taken place" (Luke 21:32 RSV). What generation was the Master talking about? Without doubt, He was talking about the generation of people who see these awesome signs of the end time, especially the troubles met by the rebuilt state of Israel. The people who see the prophecies related to the days immediately before the appearance of the Lord from heaven will be those who will be alive to be caught up into the clouds at His coming.

The Manner of His Coming

For much too long a time well-meaning Christians have argued strongly that the Second Coming of Christ is to be understood in a figurative, spiritualized way. To speak of the *parousia* as an event yet to take place at a precise point in time when the whole world must reckon with a returned Christ is a thought repugnant to some. In an ingenious attempt to get around the biblical prophecy regarding the return of Christ as King, the Christian community has created several fanciful interpretations.

Persons who do not know the Scriptures well are often heard to say that the Second Coming of Jesus has already taken place. The Lord returned on the day of Pentecost in the person of the Holy Spirit. Clearly the New Testament teaches that the Holy Spirit must be distinguished from Christ. Shortly before His death our Lord spoke of the Spirit who would come at Pentecost as the One "who proceeds from the Father" and promised that He would "bear witness to me [Christ]" (John 15:26 RSV). Just prior to this word is another in which Jesus calls the Holy Spirit "another Counselor" (14:16 RSV). Surely the term *another* means someone other than the Lord. Furthermore, all the New

Testament was written after the day of Pentecost and yet it invariably speaks of the *parousia* as a future event. Not a single New Testament writer as much as hints that the Second Coming was over and consigned to some past moment in history.

Conveniently, a neat little explanation has been put forward by those who would relegate the doctrine of the Second Advent to the time of the believer's death. This would mean that the event is repetitious and contingent upon man's experience. Nowhere does the Bible say that Christ comes to us at death. To be sure, He assured His disciples that He would be with them "even to the end of the world" (Matthew 28:20), but this was a promise of continued support for the believer which has nothing to do with a special divine coming at death. We would be more in line with the general tenor of the Christian revelation if death were conceived of as a *going to* Christ rather than as a *coming of* Christ to man. All of us are accustomed to hearing the fourteenth chapter of John used at funerals. While it is not wrong to read these words under such circumstances, the Messianic promise, ". . . I will come again and receive you unto myself" (John 14:3) is not yet fulfilled. It will happen at the *parousia*.

As if this were not enough, some have also insisted that Jesus comes every time we meet to worship. "Where two or three are gathered together in my name, there am I in the midst of them" (Matthew 18:20). There is no mention here, however, about an actual *coming*. On the contrary, it is the same truth which has been observed above in relation to the *continuous* presence of the Lord in an undergirding way. The daily consciousness of His presence with us must not be mistaken for the unique *appearance* of Christ in the clouds.

Emphatically the Bible speaks again and again of a visible bodily return of Jesus Christ to the earth. According to Hal Lindsey in *The Late Great Planet Earth* (page 171) over three hundred prophecies of his First Coming are found in the Old Testament, plus at least five hundred on the Second Coming. René Pache in *The Return of Jesus Christ* (translated by W. S. LaSor, page 5) finds far more: 1527 passages in the Old Testament and 319 in the New relating to his Second Coming.

Every one of these prophecies in the Old Testament about his First

Coming was *literally* fulfilled. Many of the prophecies in both the Old and New Testament which point to His Second Coming have come to pass already. And there is no reason to assume anything other than that every prophecy of the return of the Lord will likewise be also *literally* fulfilled.

As the disciples stood on the Mount of Olives watching anxiously the Ascension of Jesus, an angelic messenger assured them, ". . . This Jesus, who was taken up from you into heaven, will come in the same way as you saw him go into heaven" (Acts 1:11 RSV). The disciples *saw* their Lord ascend. His was a bodily form which rose from the earth and vanished from human sight. But He is not gone forever. One day we will see Him come again "in the same way" as those early followers watched Him depart. And when He comes every Christian believer will be caught up into the clouds to meet Him and join the resurrected dead who instantly precede them.

Archetypes of the Coming Lift-Off

Genesis tells the story of the translation of Enoch (Genesis 5:21–24) and a similar incident in the life of Elijah is recorded in 2 Kings 2:9–12. In the letter to the Hebrew Christians we find a reference to the first of these two godly men of old.

> By faith Enoch was taken up [translated] so that he should not see death; and he was not found, because God had taken him. Now before he was taken he was attested as having pleased God.
>
> Hebrews 11:5 RSV

Let us look for a moment at this lone, holy man who lived in a time of incomparable wickedness before the Great Flood. Succinctly his story is told in the book of beginnings: "All the days of Enoch were three hundred and sixty-five years. Enoch walked with God; and he was not; for God took him" (Genesis 5:23, 24). According to the Mosaic account, this man served God faithfully and was rewarded by being translated (removed or transferred from this earth to the heavenly sphere with the Lord). He was *caught up* and thus escaped the awful Flood which was soon to come upon the ancient world as judgment on its exceeding wickedness and corruption. For reasons unknown to us, God rewarded Elijah for his faithful prophecy in the same way. Perhaps it was because Elijah must appear as one of two witnesses in the coming tribulation (Revelation 11:4–12; cf. Malachi 4:5; Matthew 17:3). The two witnesses (the other of which is probably Moses whose death is shrouded in mystery), will be killed during that awful time. No man should have to die twice!

Both Enoch and Elijah were early types of the translation of the Church which must soon come to pass. But we must not overlook Noah whose times are compared by Jesus to the days of the Coming of the Lord (Matthew 24:36–39). Before the Flood, while the men and women around him continued in their corruption and made fun of anyone who believed in a coming deluge of water, Noah remained faithful. He was obedient to God in building the ark even though everybody was sure that he was wrong. Refusing to have any part in the godless and debauched practices of his pagan neighbors, the fearless servant of the Lord warned everyone whom he saw to repent and enter the ark. The evil was so entrenched, however, that there were no converts save his own family.

When the rains began to fall and the underground water systems overflowed their bounds, Noah and the seven members of his family entered the boat which God had told him to build. Judgment fell in death upon the peoples who had laughed without repentance, the multitudes who had jeered as they listened to this honest man's preaching. But Noah and his family were *caught up* above the terrible judgment meted out to a world of unbelief. Safely housed in their boat with the Lord they outrode the storm of God's wrath. Jehovah had lifted up His own and spared them the fearful hour of tragedy.

Enoch, Elijah, and Noah are all archetypes of the coming lift-off of the people of God. Another man named Methuselah is also a rather interesting type at whom we will look later. In each of these men can be seen similarities to that grand and glorious event which is so rapidly moving toward launch date. It may be that God has given us examples like Enoch to show how it can happen—how suddenly and permanently. If it happened to one man then it can happen to millions of men today. And if this thought alarms and frightens us it is likely that we do not

share the joyous hope of the early Christians. It was at the conclusion
of Paul's vivid description of what we have been talking about in this
chapter that he said, ". . . comfort one another with these words" (1
Thessalonians 4:18).

Effect Upon Overpopulation

By now it must have become obvious to us that this book is more
about prophecy than it is about either population or pollution. This does
not alter the fact that overpopulation and its related problems are all
bound up in the total plan of God. At the very time when overcrowded
conditions on the earth are becoming intolerable the Lord will thin out
the masses in His own way. There will be a relieving of the situation for
the world by the exit of millions of the Lord's people. The problems on
the earth will afterwards become increasingly worse, but at least there
will be a temporary respite to the population problem. If the removal
of the Church did nothing else for the unbelievers left behind, it should
convince them that God does have solutions to inescapable riddles
which human ingenuity cannot handle.

All through the New Testament we are led to believe that Christians
are a minority group. In every generation the Christian community has
been less than half the world's population (except when the Emperor
Constantine made it the state religion). When it is admitted that the
larger percentage of churchmen are only nominal Christians, it begins
to look like the prediction of Jesus was *literally* true. "For the gate is
narrow and the way is hard, that leads to life, and those who find it are
few" (Matthew 7:14 RSV). Yet, John sees a great multitude which no
man can number (Revelation 7:9) in the coming Kingdom. There is no
contradiction here at all. In every generation the redeemed are in the
minority but when those of all the ages are brought together in the end
of the age the throng will be numberless except to God who numbers
even the hairs on our heads (Luke 12:7).

Though believers living at the time of our Lord's coming may be far
smaller in number than the apostate church of the twentieth century
is ready to admit, there will still be a sizeable number of persons suddenly
evacuated. If the Saviour should come today and only 5 percent of the

world's population were ready to meet Him, the crowd would still be nearly two hundred million. That would make a noticeable difference in the people bulge.

Not only would such a *lifting out* of the people of the Lord reduce the living population, but it would also ease the problem of having inadequate burial grounds. Great numbers of graves would be abandoned and left vacant for new tenants. The redeemed of two thousand years would take leave of their cramped burial chambers for the meeting in the air. Can anyone begin to conceive of how many would be included in history's greatest grave robbery? No wonder the throngs seen by John were like the stars in number!

Only One Way to Survive

Thinning the world's peoples creates a little breathing room—but not for long. In the seven years to follow the full force of satanic wrath will be unleashed upon the remaining citizens of the world. The only way to survive is to be prepared when the Lord comes. Did not Jesus insist on the importance of such preparedness when He said, ". . . be ready; for the Son of man is coming at an hour when you do not expect" (Matthew 24:44 RSV). None can miss the point of the parable of the ten virgins. It is an admonition not to be foolishly unprepared when the bridegroom (Christ) comes, but to "Watch . . . for you know neither the day nor the hour" (25:13 RSV). One of two things must happen to every person when the Lord returns—either he enters into the joy and festivity of the marriage of the Lamb or he is left forever outside.

Writing to the Thessalonian believers, Paul warns of the sudden and unannounced appearing of Jesus "like a thief in the night" and insists that Christians "are not in darkness" so that that day surprise them (1 Thessalonians 5:2, 4). Another way of putting it is to insist that true believers will not be caught off guard because they walk in the light of the Spirit and expect the *parousia* at any moment. And to state it in reverse manner, to argue against His return or to ignore its imminence is to reveal that one is in the darkness and unprepared for the event toward which all history moves.

In following sections of this book we shall look at what those who are left on the earth following the translation of the Church will have to face. It will be seen that existence on this planet after the Church is gone will be all but impossible. Of course, some form of the apostate church will still be in operation with its ecclesiastical hierarchy in league with the enemies of God. The way to survive is to *be ready* for the coming in the clouds and the reunion of the children of God in blessed and glorious deliverance. The King is coming and His reward for the redeemed in Christ will be the fulfillment of the divine plan for those whom He knows and loves.

4
A Reason for Divine Evacuation

How It All Started

To understand the origin, mission, and destiny of the Christian Church one must go all the way back to the beginning of time. Unless the divine panorama of biblical history is seen in its entirety there is no conceivable way to properly grasp the meaning of the Church. Without seeing the locus of the *ecclesia* (Greek New Testament word for *church* meaning "the called out") in its total historical context, we are like men looking at only a fragmentation of the divine picture. Since this is so manifest as to require no further insistence, let us take a moment to trace the acts of God in developing His plan from Eden to Pentecost.

One created being was already on the earth before the appearance of man. In the Old Testament he is called *Lucifer* (Isaiah 14:12–15). He had been originally created by God as the head of the angelic beings who served before the Lord. The prophet describes him as "the anointed cherub that covereth" (Ezekiel 28:14) which probably has to do with his angelic headship and general surveillance of the newly-made world. Being given this exalted position of authority, which made him second only to God Himself, was too much even for an angel. Thus we encounter the origin of evil in the rebellion of Lucifer and his resultant expulsion from the heavenly abode of God. This accounts for Satan's (the New Testament name for Lucifer) presence in the Garden of Eden and his subtle tactics used to interfere with the Creator's plan.

Adam and Eve were created without sin and placed in a new world of innocent purity. In a sense, man was the divine replacement of Lucifer in a different dimension of existence. Adam was to be God's chosen servant, even closer to Him than the angels, and was to be given dominion over the whole earth (Genesis 1:26). Everything was to be under his surveillance and authority including all other living creatures as well as the actual land itself. But Satan seduced the woman, who in turn seduced the man, to do things his way rather than God's. In the human surrender to the tempter the scepter of dominion was wrested from man and controlled by Lucifer. Thus Satan assumed the role of "god of this world" (2 Corinthians 4:4) and man's long struggle began —a battle which continues to this day.

As would be expected, the ancient world grew exceedingly wicked as it followed the leading of man's chosen god. No one was in a position to be a mediator between the world's peoples and the world's Creator because sin had rendered the entire race incapable of access to God. The result was that the situation grew worse until the world was "corrupt and over-run with violence" (Genesis 6:11 RSV). Ultimately, the plight of man became so desperate and the plan of God so completely perverted that the Flood of divine judgment wiped the surface of the world clean of human life. Only one family was left to make a fresh start.

After the flood had subsided, God renewed the original dominion of man for Noah (9:2). This one man, out of all who had lived, could be trusted to carry out the divine design. Once more the Lord would seek to rule the human race through Noah and specially chosen descendants. But, alas, as men began to multiply again they forgot God and, under the subtle strategy of the "god of this world," decided to construct a universal kingdom for themselves without regard to the rule of the Lord. The Tower of Babel was the symbol of their rebellion and self-sufficiency (Genesis 11:1–9). Though God did not destroy the human race as had been the remedy used earlier, He broke up their little plot and settled them in divisive nations as a punishment for their ecumenical self-sufficiency.

The Founding of a Nation

Telescoping His sights on a more limited area of mankind, God called one man out of the cradle of civilization in Ur to be the father of a chosen people through whom "all families of the earth shall bless themselves" (Genesis 12:3 RSV). His name was Abraham and the covenant which God made with him was to be "an everlasting possession" (17:8) of the land of Canaan as the home of a select people. The long-range purpose of God was to mold and sensitize a people after His own will out of whom the "seed [of the woman]" (3:15) destined to defeat Satan could arise. That one was to be the King who would reign in righteousness as the second Adam (1 Corinthians 15:45–47). Through Him the whole world would be restored to its primeval state which existed before the Fall.

The mills of the Lord grind slowly. After three hundred years the descendants of Abraham found themselves in bondage in the land of Egypt. Their hard lot there for over four hundred years taught them how to face hardship. Eventually, when God was ready to deliver them, He chose Moses to be the human instrument of negotiation with Pharaoh. The miracles which the Lord manifested by Moses, especially the bloodbath on the night of the Passover (Exodus 12), would convince them of the power of their God and their dependence on Him. In the defeat of Pharaoh's intent to restrain the Hebrews from leaving and throughout the forty years of wilderness wandering after the Exodus, Moses was the mediator chosen by God to speak for the Lord and to intercede for the people. Already the problem of creating a nation of faithful men was beginning to appear. Murmuring, questioning, complaining, disbelief— this was why it took forty years to get from Egypt to Canaan!

At Sinai it was necessary to initiate laws by which the new kingdom would live (Exodus 20). It was the divine intention that this new endeavor would result in "a kingdom of priests and an holy nation" (19:6) and for this reason the laws of the Mosaic covenant were given. In the keeping of these laws and the devoted service to God, the Hebrews would set such an example that all nations would come to her light.

In the Book of Joshua we are told how the Lord gave the land of Canaan into the possession of the Hebrews as had been promised to Abraham nearly a millennium before. Wise men and women known as judges were appointed to settle disputes and reconcile problems in the early days of the nation. It was not long, however, until the people of God demanded a king like the pagan nations around them which grew out of the dispersed conditions that developed after the Tower of Babel incident (1 Samuel 8:5). Of course, this displeased not only Samuel but

God as well. It was an indication that the nation wanted to depend on human rule more than on divine rule. Of interest is the fact that the Lord, though displeased, is willing to give man a chance to assume a larger share in the handling of the nation's affairs. We are told that "the Lord hath set a king over you" (12:13).

First to be inaugurated as king was Saul, whose leadership degenerated to the point of personal despair and suicide (31:4). The second ruler was specially picked by God. His name was David and under his reign Israel was to enjoy her finest hours. The promise which God made to David reiterated the terms of the Abrahamic covenant and further established a throne in David's line which would never end. ". . . thine house and thy kingdom shall be established for ever before thee: thy throne shall be established for ever" (2 Samuel 7:16). And it was through this kingly line that the long-awaited Anointed One would ultimately come.

God's Plan for a Kingdom Falls Apart

Israel's power and prominence began to enter into eclipse toward the end of the reign of David's son, Solomon, who became much too intent on pagan alliances and a growing harem of wives and concubines. At his death, the kingdom broke apart under the uprising of Jeroboam, an Ephraimite, who set up a separate nation in the north with ten of the twelve tribes. Ahijah, the prophet, had predicted earlier that the kingdom would be divided (1 Kings 11:30–35) and Jeroboam would be the first ruler of the Northern Kingdom, still to be known as Israel, with its capital at Samaria. Rehoboam, son of Solomon, continued the Davidic line in a new Southern Kingdom called Judah with its king's palace at Jerusalem.

Nineteen kings were to reign in Israel and nineteen in Judah until moral and spiritual degeneracy brought an end to the Northern confederation in 721 B.C. and to the Southern Kingdom in 586 B.C. Israel was beseiged, conquered, and carried into captivity by Assyria. Judah was conquered by Babylon in a devastating defeat in which the Holy City of David was sacked and destroyed including the Temple of the Lord. God's plan to form a holy nation had fallen apart, but the kingdom promised to Abraham and the throne given to David were yet to survive.

In His own inimitable way, God would gather a Remnant of the faithful in Babylon and return them to rebuild the Temple and the walls of Jerusalem. The kingdom, however, would "be no more until he come whose right it is: and I will give it to him" (Ezekiel 21:27; cf. Daniel 7:13, 14; Hosea 3:4, 5; Luke 1:32, 33). One must recall at this point that the founding of the kingdom in the first place was to produce the King who would carry out God's plan. That King was to be Jesus, "the seed of the woman."

Following the fall of Judah, the kingdom of David, God turned the rule of the world over to four successive Gentile empires known to history as Babylon, Medo-Persia, Greece, and Rome. A detailed prediction of each of these ruling peoples is preserved for us in the second and seventh chapters of the prophetic Book of Daniel. This period of Gentile rule from the fall of Judah to the coming of Christ the second time is called "the times of the Gentiles" (Luke 21:24). Under the Persian rule of Cyrus, the Remnant was permitted to return to Jerusalem (2 Chronicles 36:22, 23; Ezra 1:2, 3) where the little nation later struggled under the oppression of Greek dominance. Rome, who was next to control Israel, must be given credit for treating the Jewish people with great leniency in regard to their religious convictions. And it was in the midst of this situation that the Heir to David's throne was to appear.

The King Is Born

Seven hundred years before the birth of Jesus, the prophet Isaiah had announced, "O house of David . . . the Lord himself shall give you a sign; Behold, a virgin shall conceive, and bear a son, and shall call his name Immanuel" (Isaiah 7: 13, 14). The same prophet revealed that this child would bear the government of Israel upon his shoulder and be called "Wonderful Counselor, Mighty God, Everlasting Father, Prince of Peace." Furthermore, of His kingdom "there will be no end" and it shall be established "with justice and righteousness from this time forth and for ever more . . ." (Isaiah 9:6, 7 RSV). Micah also saw the day when, out of Bethlehem, would "come forth for me [God] one who is to be ruler in Israel, whose reign is from of old, from ancient days" (Micah 5:2).

For four hundred years the voice of the prophet had been silent in the land. The night had grown so dark that something had to happen. In fact, the entire world was at this time in history looking for a Saviour. There could have been no period more ripe for the advent of the King. Even the sudden appearance of John the Baptist, reminiscent of the prophets of old, added to the feeling that something great was about to happen. His message was "Repent, for the kingdom of heaven is at hand" (Matthew 3:2). John was dead certain that the King was coming: ". . . he who is coming after me is mightier than I . . . His winnowing fork is in his hand, and he will clear his threshing floor and gather his wheat into the granary, but the chaff he will burn with unquenchable fire" (3:11, 12).

Just as God had spoken through His prophets of old, so it happened on that night in Bethlehem when the Holy Family had gone to be taxed in the great census. In a stable of hay came Him to whom the throne of David belonged. Through Mary, descendant of Nathan, son of David, Jesus was "the seed of the woman" promised in the Garden of Eden. And through His adopted father, Joseph, descendant of Solomon, son of David, He was the long-awaited King. Thus, the angelic hosts sang in the heavens over the stable where Jesus lay, "Glory to God in the highest, and on earth peace among men with whom he is pleased" (Luke 2:14 RSV). And lest there be any doubt about the identity of the babe, an angel said to the frightened shepherds, "Be not afraid; for behold, I bring you news of a great joy which will come to all the people; for to you is born this day in the City of David a Savior, who is Christ the Lord" (Luke 2:10, 11 RSV).

The King Is Rejected

Everywhere Jesus went during His three years of preaching and teaching ministry, He announced the Kingdom as did John the Baptist, ". . . Repent: for the kingdom of heaven is at hand" (Matthew 4:17). When the Twelve were sent out on their mission, Jesus clearly stated, ". . . Go nowhere among the Gentiles, and enter no town of the Samaritans, but go rather to the lost sheep of the house of Israel. And preach as you go saying, 'The kingdom of heaven is at hand' " (Matthew 10:5–7 RSV). Luke records a similar charge given to the Seventy, a charge to announce, ". . . The kingdom of God has come near to you' " (Luke 10:9 RSV).

On the Sunday before His Crucifixion, Jesus rode on a lowly beast into the City of David. Such a dramatic act was a clear claim to being the Messiah. Zechariah had prophesied that the Heir to David's throne would come "triumphant and victorious . . . humble and riding on an ass . . ." (Zechariah 9:9 RSV) and Matthew relates the events of Palm Sunday to that prophecy (Matthew 21:5). The crowds sensed the royal aura which surrounded the man on the donkey and shouted en masse, "Hosanna to the Son of David! Blessed is he who comes in the name of the Lord! Hosanna in the highest!" (Matthew 21:9 RSV). When the High Priest demanded whether Jesus were the Christ (Messiah or King designate), the Lord replied, "You have said so . . ." (26:64 RSV). The same answer was given to Pilate when the governor asked, "Are you the King of the Jews?" (27:11 RSV). On the titulus over the cross were inscribed the words, THIS IS THE KING OF THE JEWS (Luke 23:38 RSV).

The Kingdom of Israel was offered that day to the Jewish nation on the condition that the people accept their King. But the people cried out, "Crucify him! . . . We have no king but Caesar" (John 19:15 RSV). Within hours Jesus was on the cross and the universe was furious. Thunder and lightning shattered the sky as darkness fell upon the nation. God had had enough! The veil of the Temple was torn apart, the earth trembled, rocks were shattered, and tombs were opened (Matthew 27:51–53).

A chosen people whom the Lord had been preparing since the call of Abraham two thousand years earlier had rejected God's best—His own Son. In so doing, they had refused their King and forfeited their last chance to restore the Kingdom of David. There could be no Kingdom without a King! It would be a long time before the Lord would come again with an offer like that, but come He would. And the next time it would be more than an offer—it would be a rule with an iron hand. James recalls the prophet's words given him by the King Himself, "After this I will return and I will rebuild the dwelling of David, which has fallen . . ." (Acts 15:16 RSV). Nothing could be clearer. The King is coming again. No one has said it better than the writer of Hebrews:

. . . he has appeared once for all at the end of the age to put away sin by the sacrifice of himself. And just as it is appointed for men to die once, and after that comes judgment, so Christ, having been offered once to bear the sins of many, will appear a second time, not to deal with sin but to save those who are eagerly waiting for him.

Hebrews 9:26–28 RSV

The reference, of course, is to the Church who is "eagerly waiting for him" in His return with clouds to catch away His believing disciples. This is where the translation of the Church fits into the picture. Let us look more closely now at the reason for this evacuation in light of what has been seen thus far in our running history of the Kingdom of Israel.

An Interlude in Time

Philosophical theologians have duped multitudes of people within the institutional church into believing that the Church is a continuation of the Kingdom of Israel. This makes the Kingdom and the Church one and the same thing. Never has there been a greater deception foisted upon the followers of Christ than this. Nowhere does the Bible support such a theory. When one departs from the pure Word of God for the ambiguous opinions of men, he is in trouble. Philosophical theology is centered in man's judgment. Biblical theory is rooted in God's wisdom. They do not start at the same place nor do they end at the same destination.

The Church, far from being equated with the Kingdom of Israel, was completely unknown in the Old Testament. None of the prophets mention it except Daniel and he simply envisions a break in the prophetic timetable which he does not understand (Daniel 9). The Church is a mystery which the Hebrews never conceived. Thus when it came into existence on the day of Pentecost, they neither understood it nor knew what to do about it. Jesus spoke of the unfolding mystery as "My Church" and announced to His disciples that He would "build it" (Matthew 16:18), a certainty that it was to be something brand new. Nowhere is the Church spoken of as something to be *rebuilt* or *restored* like the fallen Kingdom. Rather, it is to be built new as a kind of parenthesis between the Hebrew rejection of the Messiah and the Messiah's coming again to restore the Kingdom of Israel.

Paul deals with this *mystery* in his epistle to the church at Ephesus. He discusses the new relationship between our Lord and those who believe in Him in chapter two. But it is in the next chapter where the specific mystery is mentioned three times. This mystery has been revealed to the apostle but it ". . . was not made known to the sons of men in other generations as it has now been revealed to his holy apostles and prophets by the Spirit; that is, how the Gentiles are fellow heirs, members of the same body, and partakers of the promise in Christ Jesus through the gospel" (Ephesians 3:5, 6 RSV). Paul goes on to insist that he was commissioned to "make all men see what is the plan of the mystery hidden for ages in God who created all things; that through the church the manifold wisdom of God might now be made known to the principalities and powers in the heavenly places" (3:9, 10 RSV). Manifestly, the mystery involves the unmerited favor of God by which persons outside the covenant with Abraham were now invited to share equally with Jews. The basis on which the equality rests is belief in the death and Resurrection of Christ as Saviour and Lord (Colossians 1:- 24–28).

We do well to remember that the *ecclesia* is "the called out" people of Christ. When the Hebrew nation rejected the Kingdom of the Lord, God turned to the Gentiles (Greek word is *ethnos* which means *nations*) with an invitation to enter into a spiritual relationship issuing in eternal life. "Simeon hath declared how God at first did visit the Gentiles, to take out of them a people for his name" (Acts 15:14). The Church is a special group chosen to be "the Bride of Christ" (Revelation 21:2) who will share the rule of the Bridegroom when He comes to reign during the Millennium. Being the Bride, the Church is under grace, not under law as were the Jews who were citizens of a kingdom. The Bride will be members of the family of God sharing the glory of the ruling Son. This being so, the translation of the Church is necessary in order to consummate the marriage and be prepared for the resumption of the Messianic Kingdom.

Long ago Daniel envisioned a break in the dealings of God with the

Davidic Kingdom (Daniel 9:24–27). He saw the entire period of Israel's history from the date of the rebuilding of the city of Jerusalem in the fifth century before Christ to the reign of Antichrist. The prophetic reference is to a total of seventy weeks (*shebua* in Hebrew meaning seven, thus each week equals seven years) which gives a total of four hundred ninety weeks. On the basis of events which have transpired, each of the weeks further represents a year in time. Sixty-nine weeks clearly covered the period from the rebuilding of the city to the first advent of Christ. Between week sixty-nine and week seventy there was envisioned a time when the Messiah would be "cut off." This is the rejection of the King by the Jews, His crucifixion, and the attendant tragedies which befell the nation by the time of its final collapse in A.D. 70. It represented the prolonged period of the Church interlude which began with the death of the Saviour. At the end of the Church age Daniel sees a final week of terrible events in the life of the nation. These events under a false Messiah are undoubtedly the same as those described in Revelation as the seven years of great tribulation in the reign of Antichrist (Revelation 11–21).

Atonement for the Nations

For over nineteen hundred years the world has been in the midst of the Church age, the period between the last two prophetic weeks which is of undetermined duration. How much longer it can last, no one knows, not "even the angels of heaven, nor the Son, but the Father only" (Matthew 24:36 RSV). Increasing fulfillment of Biblical signs of the end would indicate that "the times of the Gentiles" are about to run out. Soon the Lord will appear and remove His Church. That will bring an end to the Church age. While it lasts, however, the saving grace of our Lord Jesus Christ is accessible for the nations.

Nowhere in the Old Testament covenant was the Gentile provided an atonement for sin. Atonement was for the Jewish nation alone and it was sought by the High Priest on one special day during each year. Only then did he enter into the Holy of Holies to sacrifice for the people. When the veil which shrouded that holy place was rent as Christ died on the cross, notice was given to the whole world that any man—Jew or Gentile—now had access to God through Christ's sacrifice (Hebrews 7:25–27). The sacrificial system had come to its end for Christ was "the Lamb of God who takes away the sin of the world" (John 1:29 RSV). Isaiah foresaw that sacrificial work when he wrote of the Suffering Servant, He is "like a lamb that is led to the slaughter" (Isaiah 53:7 RSV). And the Corinthian letter of Paul insists that "our paschal lamb has been sacrificed" (1 Corinthians 5:7 RSV).

Devout Jews had trusted their High Priest to obtain forgiveness for them as they obeyed God's demand for a sacrifice of blood, a symbol of returning the life to the Creator from whence it came. Christ became man's High Priest as well as the sacrifice as He died on the cross. Atonement is now available for all people as a result of that day of Atonement observed nineteen hundred years ago. During this twenty-century interval of time men and women, whether Jew or Gentile, need only to trust our High Priest who has obtained forgiveness for us by the sacrifice of Himself. This is what is so significant in Paul's classic challenge to the jailer, ". . . Believe on the Lord Jesus Christ and thou shalt be saved. . ." (Acts 16:31).

This then is the meaning and purpose of the interlude in prophetic history known as the Church age or "the times of the Gentiles." God has been *calling out* a people for Himself who will be the Bride for His Son. The Ephesian letter sums up in beautiful fashion the divine plan for the mystery of the ages, the Church of our Lord.

> . . . Christ loved the church and gave himself up for her [a reference to what God *has done* in the death of the Saviour], that he might sanctify her, having cleansed her by the washing of water with the word [a clear statement about what He is *now doing* during this Church age], that he might present the church to himself in splendor, without spot or wrinkle or any such thing, that she might be holy and without blemish [a precise explanation as to what He *will do* for the Church at the translation].
>
> Ephesians 5:25–27 RSV

When the allotted time for the Gentiles is ended and the task of the Church is completed, God will say, "Everybody out!" With no reason for any more delay, the righteous dead will come out of their graves and the living believers will come out of the world order. It will be the grandest "coming-out party" in history when Jesus presents His Bride to the Father for divine approval and blessing. That is the "blessed hope" (Titus 2:13) for which the Church has been looking since the Ascension of its Lord. Today, as never before, we are hearing the words of the Lord Jesus, "Surely I am coming soon." And to His words we respond, "Amen. Come Lord Jesus!" (Revelation 22:20 RSV).

The State of the Church After Translation

The Church has nothing to do with the Kingdom of Israel. During this time of grace we who are Christians are to witness to both Jew and Gentile of the saving power of Jesus Christ. We are to "go . . . and make disciples of all nations" (Matthew 28:19 RSV) that the Church may finally be complete at the coming of the Lord. But the Church will never be a part of the actual Kingdom of Israel. The two are totally different and mutually exclusive. And since the *ecclesia* (the called out) have not been included in the Abrahamic covenant nor have they shared in the rejection of a Kingdom, it stands to reason that they will not figure in the troubles destined for the final days of the Jewish nation. It is certain that the State of Israel, which has been lately reestablished, will face the most severe troubles in its ancient history. The troubles, according to prophecy of both Old and New Testaments, will engage the entire world and result in the final battle of Armageddon and the end of the age. Therefore, if the Church is to be spared this "time of Jacob's trouble" (Jeremiah 30:7; *see also* Zechariah 13:8, 9) it is needful that the Lord remove it from the scene.

Several references are made in the gospels to "the marriage supper of the Lamb" (Revelation 19:9). The parable of the ten virgins is definitely Messianic and eschatological (end time) and has to do with the privilege to be enjoyed by the Church after the *parousia* (Matthew 25:1–13). There is also a story about a king who "gave a marriage feast for his son" (Matthew 22:1–14 RSV). Certainly, the motif of the Church as "the Bride of Christ" and the many similar references to a marriage feast belong together. Our Lord is coming for His Church and together we

will enjoy the festivities of the marriage supper during the interval of
Antichrist's rule upon the earth. The scene is depicted aptly for us by
John:

". . . Let us rejoice and exult and give him the glory,
for the marriage of the Lamb has come,
and his Bride has made herself ready;
it was granted to her to be clothed with fine linen, bright and pure"—
for the fine linen is the righteous deeds of the saints.
    And the angel said to me, "Write this: Blessed are those who are
invited to the marriage supper of the Lamb."

Revelation 19:7–9 RSV

After the troubles on earth are past and the marriage supper is ended,
Christ will return to the earth "with all his saints" (1 Thessalonians 3:13)
where they will enjoy the thousand-year reign of peace with Him who
is the Prince of Peace. But during that seven years of awful tribulation
on the earth, the redeemed will spend their time in heavenly places as
those who experience one grand and glorious time of feasting, festivity,
and fellowship with Christ and each other.

5
Post Lift-Off Troubles

Missing: One True Church

When we speak of troubles after the translation, we are not thinking of the Church. Those hard times which have beset the Christian community will be over. Here on the earth, however, troubles will have just begun. The conditions on the earth will revert to a situation similar to that which existed prior to the Great Flood when there was no mediator between God and man and when the earth was steeped in corruption and violence. If the disorder and violence, revolution, and anarchy of our time seem threatening to us, then we had better not think about the future or we shall succumb to heart failure! Life in the world will grow rapidly worse—like a mounting crescendo—until the end comes.

In every generation since the days of Christ the Church has served as the conscience of society. Often the conscience has been weak due to the degenerate state of the ecclesiastical institution. But, at least, such an institution has reminded men and women of the need for ethics and responsibility toward God and one's fellow men. What is even more important than that, in the midst of times of deep apostasy there have always been a few who stood tall for God. In the presence of these people of God the world has been held in check against the kind of open wickedness which would have prevailed in its absence.

Christians are "the salt of the earth" (Matthew 5:13). It is they who keep the world from going completely bad. There is a purifying quality about redeemed members of the Body of Christ which serves as a cathartic for the poison being spread through masses of fallen men in high places. Few would argue that Christians have not been responsible for preserving the world from destruction long overdue for our wickedness. In a very real way, the true Church has restrained the hand of divine judgment on a deserving planet of rebellious creatures. Chaos and irrevocable destruction would have come long ago if the Christian Church were not at work as a purifying and preserving agent.

Jesus further emphasized that His disciples are to be "the light of the world" (Matthew 5:14). On numerous occasions in the past we have witnessed the darkness of evil as it settled upon the world's peoples. One period in history is remembered as The Dark Ages and even the period called The Enlightenment was filled with nether gloom due to our tragically false concept of the nature of man. But the darkness witnessed in the years now gone was as the noonday sun compared to the midnight forces to be unleashed upon the earth following the evacuation of the world by the Church. Jesus was the world's "true Light" (John 1:9). When He was crucified, darkness fell upon the nation of Israel for three hours in the middle of the day. During the interval of time while the Lord is away from the earth in the flesh, Christians are charged with the responsibility of being the light. And when the Church is finally removed the light will be gone completely! Manifestly, we are talking about the light of conscience and truth. Later we will see how God restores a faint ray of hope for persons who will believe in those dark times.

Our Lord further likened the mystery of the Church age to "leaven, which a woman took, and hid in three measures of meal, till the whole was leavened" (Matthew 13:33). This simply meant that the Church is to infiltrate the world with the leavening of the gospel. Leaven is often used in an evil sense in the New Testament (see Luke 12:1), but it can describe a good process of inner change as well. God's Church has been commissioned to preach, instruct, heal, and serve in every area of the world's life until the gospel of redemption has leavened mankind and all his organized structures. When the leaven is no more present among men the conditions on earth will be of such hopeless nature as to bring about the total collapse of the world order—like bread without a change agent such as yeast.

For nearly twenty centuries the Christian Church has been despised and persecuted. This is not always true in its outward manifestations of institutional life. When the organized Church compromises with pagan cultural values it is not persecuted, just ignored. But in its inward life

of commitment to the saving Christ the true Church becomes a conscience for a people bent on secular existence (living as though there is
no God) and is inevitably despised. The day will come when this situation will be reversed. Once the Church is gone from man's world,
multitudes will recognize what the Christian community has meant to
human existence and will regret its disappearance. When the newspapers carry the story: MILLIONS OF CHRISTIANS DISAPPEAR FROM THE
WORLD, those left behind will be destined for calamity upon calamity.
The population may be considerably decreased, but those who are still
here cannot possibly profit by it!

Israel to be Continued

Numerous prophecies in the Old Testament can only be understood
in light of a restoration of the nation of Israel in full Kingdom power
which was not realized in the return of the Remnant from Babylon. We
can only look at a few of them here. Isaiah leaves no ambiguity in our
minds when he says:

> And it shall come to pass in that day, that the Lord shall set his
> hand again the second time to recover the remnant of his people,
> which shall be left, from Assyria, and from Egypt, and from Pa-
> thros, and from Cush, and from Elam, and from Shinar, and from
> Hamath, and from the islands of the sea.
>
> Isaiah 11:11

That sounds rather emphatic and clear. Not until the last half of the
twentieth century has this prophecy been fulfilled even in a remote way.
In the following verse the prophet continues, "And he shall set up an
ensign for the nations, and shall assemble the outcasts of Israel, and
gather together the dispersed of Judah from the four corners of the
earth" (Isaiah 11:12). Both the ten tribes of Israel and the Davidic
Kingdom of Judah are included in this forecast and they shall be gleaned
out of the nineteen-hundred year dispersion "from the four corners of
the earth." That must mean a general restoration involving the farthest
reaches of the world. And that did not happen when the Jews returned
from captivity in Babylon.

Ezekiel, in the famous story of the resurrection of dry bones, hears the Lord affirming:

> And I will make them one nation in the land upon the mountains of Israel; and one king shall be king to them all: and they shall be no more two nations, neither shall they be divided into two kingdoms anymore at all . . . And they shall dwell in the land that I have given unto Jacob my servant, wherein your fathers have dwelt; and they shall dwell therein, even they, and their children, and their children's children forever: and my servant David shall be their prince forever.
>
> Ezekiel 37:22, 25

Daniel, in his vision of the seventy weeks, sees the system of sacrifice restored to the returned nation of Israel. This would necessitate the rebuilding of the Temple. Sacrifices will be offered unto God only in such a Temple which must be erected on its original site—Mount Zion in the city of Jerusalem where the Moslem Dome of the Rock now stands. In order to accomplish this feat the Jews must be in possession of the land of Abraham including the City of David. Not until recently has this been accomplished.

Jesus warns of the end times when there will be great trouble for the Jews in their own country (*see* Matthew 24). No amount of spiritualizing the Scriptures can justifiably read anything else into these specific predictions. The Jews will be back in their land and the nation will continue as it was when the Romans destroyed it in A.D. 70. Everything will be modernized and many of the old landmarks will be destroyed in the redevelopment of an ancient city and its surrounding country. But Hebrew life, though in disbelief as regards the Messiah, will continue after nearly two thousand years of interrupted life by the interlude of the Church age.

Gentile World Supremacy Also Continued

At the time of the brutal massacre of myriads of Jews in Jerusalem and the vicious scattering of David's people into the far distant countries of the world, the mighty Roman Empire was in control of most of the civilized world. The next two hundred fifty years were to be a time of terrible persecution for the new phenomenon of the Christian Church. The Jews were to suffer also, but not in their land or in such cruel manner as did the Christians. For nineteen hundred years, however, the children of Abraham have been envied, despised, and driven all over the world. Everywhere they have gone they have prospered, but nations have treated them as outcasts, men and women without a country. During World War II over six million of them were put to death in the concentration camps of Germany.

When the Jews are restored to their nation promised to Abraham as "an everlasting possession," there will be another restoration as well. If life is to continue as though there had been no Church age interruption, the source of tension which characterized the destruction of Jerusalem in A.D. 70 must be back in force. That source of enmity was the Roman Empire. The Bible states that, in the last days, the empire of the Caesars will be restored.

Once more we must call on Daniel, the prophet whose divine inspiration and holy insight enabled him to interpret the king of Babylon's dreams. A panorama of what was to come from the prophet's day until the end of the age is preserved for us in his vision of the four beasts which emerged out of the sea (Daniel 7:1-28). There is little disagreement about the identity of the world empires symbolized by these beasts. First, he saw a lion (Babylon); second, a bear (Medo-Persia); third, a leopard (Greece); and fourth, a beast so ferocious that he could only describe its features without giving it a name (Rome). It was the last beast which ruled when Jesus was crucified and the City of David was destroyed. What Daniel predicts about the beast of Rome involves conditions which prevail until the Second Coming of Christ. In the end of the age there are seen ten kings (represented by ten horns) as the organized confederacy of the Roman Empire which, since it has not existed since the late fifth century after Christ, must be restored as Israel has been reestablished in the Land of Promise.

John the apostle, writing over a half-century after the death of Jesus, envisions the restoration of the empire of Rome in precisely the same way as did Daniel over six hundred years earlier (Revelation 17:1-18). In this chapter the apostle also sees the apostate religious institution

(depicted in "the mother of harlots") as it works in close cooperation
with the pagan empire. The "seven heads" on the beast are specifically
explained as "seven mountains" where the harlot is enthroned. Rome
was known as "the city of seven hills." One can hardly mistake the
pointed symbolism. There are "ten horns" mentioned, as in Daniel, and
they clearly represent a confederation of nations within the framework
of the restored empire. More detailed study will be undertaken in a later
section of this book. At this point, the important thing to remember is
that both the Kingdom of David and the Roman Empire are to be
restored to their respective places of power for the final conflict between
God and anti-God.

History Repeats Itself

With the Church gone from the earth, we have suggested that the
world will be again as it was in those days between murderous Cain and
the Great Flood. Jesus warned about that awful time between the
translation of the Church and the coming of the King in judgment in
Matthew's gospel.

> . . . as the days of Noe were, so shall also the coming of the Son
> of man be. For as in the days that were before the flood they were
> eating and drinking, marrying and giving in marriage, until the day
> that Noe entered into the ark, And knew not until the flood came,
> and took them all away; so shall also the coming of the Son of man
> be.
>
> Matthew 24:38, 39

The sordid picture which Jesus draws needs no additional illumina-
tion. From His graphic description can be gathered all the information
we need about the way things were before the Flood. In fact, they seem
to have been much like they are right now. All the people were going
about their secular pursuits as though they were oblivious to the existence of God and had no inkling of a disaster like a flood. Obviously,
they had grown complacent with their little game of caring for their

physical appetites. Our Lord is saying that, though this may be descriptive of almost any age to a degree, it is especially the way things will be during the tribulation. No better portrayal of life without recognition of a Supreme Ruler of the universe could be written.

Is there anything more that we can say about conditions on the earth prior to the great deluge? Probably. The Old Testament has many archetypes for persons and events later to be. In an earlier part of this book we looked briefly at some of them. A character, usually overlooked except for his age, lived during the pre-Flood period and seems to figure in it in a rather subtle way. His name was Methuselah and his nine hundred sixty-nine years had a prophetic meaning. Methuselah's father, Enoch, was the only godly man of his day—so godly that he was translated from earth to heaven. When he named his son, he chose a word which summed up his expectations for his boy. In Hebrew the name means: "When he is gone, so be it."

It is not too much to conjecture that, in those long walks together, God revealed to His servant what was soon to happen. If so, Enoch probably asked when the flood could be expected and the Lord said, "Methuselah" in reference to Enoch's son. Thus the boy became a sign of the end. When Methuselah was gone the Flood would come. We have sparse details about these antediluvians, therefore, we can only assume that Enoch told his son and Methuselah became an object lesson to the people who lived in the surrounding area. The news was bound to have gotten out by word of mouth until everybody knew about old Methuselah. Perhaps they laughed at the whole idea as they mocked the stupidity of an old man who would build a huge boat in the middle of dry land.

Some will insist that all this is conjured speculation. The interesting thing is to be found in the way things worked out. Methuselah was 187 years old when his son, Lamech, was born (Genesis 5:25) and Lamech was 182 years old when Methuselah's grandson, Noah, was born (5:28). Thus Methuselah was 369 years old at the birth of Noah. In chapter 7, where the Flood is recorded, we discover that Noah was 600 years old when the Flood came. Methuselah lived to be 969 years old. That means that he reached that hoary age the same year as the Flood destroyed the inhabitants of the old world. Apparently, he had been named right and he was a sign to the people. When he was gone, they should have gotten ready for the deluge. But they paid no attention to the sign.

Does history repeat itself? God has destroyed the world only once and He will do it only once more. As Methuselah's removal from the earth's living was a sign to the people of Noah's day, so the translation of the Church is a sign to men and women left on the earth after the lift-off! When the Church is gone, so be it! Swift judgment will fall upon all peoples and within one prophetic week (seven years) the King will return with His saints to destroy the wicked and establish His reign of peace.

A Realized Political Confederation

First, it was the Tower of Babel. In our day it has been the League of Nations and now the United Nations. In each case, plus many attempts between the construction of the ancient Tower and World War I, man sought to create some kind of world government by which peace could be insured and every nation could be kept in line with a well-defined charter. Billions of dollars are spent each year trying to avoid war by peaceful negotiations supervised by a complex body of representatives from many countries of the world. It may be true that the United Nations has forestalled a nuclear war and the destruction of civilization. This we will never know. But it is a fact that it has not eliminated war or brought a solution to the big problem which confronts the world—man himself!

Occasionally, we hear someone say that what the confused and shattered world needs now is a beneficent dictator who will rule with an iron hand. That kind of gentleman is getting to be a rare breed! But if this is what we want we are in for a shock. For a dictator is exactly what we are going to get, only he will not turn out to be the kind we expected. According to the Scriptures, in the end of the age there will arise one man who will become powerful almost overnight. He will rise to great heights and be demanded by the multitudes as the sole ruler of the whole earth. We will have our dictator and he will be the Antichrist. Both the Old Testament and the New foresaw his rise to power. John writes, ". . . and power was given him over all kindreds, and tongues, and nations" (Revelation 13:7).

Daniel envisioned the power of this one ruler who will control the whole restored Roman Empire comprised of its ten participating nations.

> I considered the horns, and behold, there came up among them another little horn [the Antichrist], before whom there were three of the first horns plucked up by the roots: and behold, in this horn were eyes like the eyes of man, and a mouth speaking great things.
>
> Daniel 7:8

Little question remains but that the United Nations—a modern Tower of Babel which seeks peace without God—is laying the necessary groundwork for the one-world government, the reins of which the coming Antichrist will easily pick up. This is not to say that the United Nations is all bad. But it is to suggest that man's rebel attempt to create one world without due regard to the need of a Saviour to change his heart is futile. And it is further to affirm that what is taking place before our eyes is the direct fulfillment of prophecy. God said it would happen because He knows fallen human nature.

It is the complexity of a world which reels to and fro like a drunken man that has brought us to the threshold of not only accepting but demanding a dictator. Anyone who thinks more than superficially will instantly recognize the impossibility of having any semblance of world government without such an all-powerful ruler. In the vision of John, where the Antichrist is portrayed as a beast in like manner as in Daniel, these unmistakable words assure us that we may anticipate the coming of this one-world government with a bestial head.

> And the ten horns which thou sawest are ten kings, which have received no kingdom as yet; but receive power as kings one hour with the beast. These have one mind, and shall give their power and strength unto the beast.
>
> Revelation 17:12, 13

A Realized Economic Unity

Under the headship of the Antichrist shall develop a worldwide system of buying and selling which is carefully controlled. No one will be able to engage in business except as he is permitted by the dictator's regime. Daniel writes, ". . .he shall cause craft to prosper. . ." (Daniel 8:25). The Book of Revelation has some very frightening things to say about the economic conditions which will prevail under the ten-nation confederacy governed by an iron-fisted dictator.

He causeth all, both small and great, rich and poor, free and bond, to receive a mark in their right hand, or in their foreheads: And that no man might buy or sell, save he that had the mark, or the name of the beast, or the number of his name.

Revelation 13:16, 17

This restored Roman Empire (over which Antichrist holds sway) will naturally be in the continent of Europe. That is where the old empire was, with its palace and headquarters at Rome, and we may be sure that the revived confederacy of nations will be located there. Several attempts have been made to unify Europe under a totalitarian form of government. Adolf Hitler is remembered best by modern man for his efforts in this direction. But there has never been any design for European unification in history to compare with the Common Market of our time. The plan is to have at least ten nations within the confederacy, countries bound together in an economic unity which would give these nations of the restored Roman Empire the edge over any other part of the world in controlling the economy in its own way.

It was following the Treaty of Rome in 1957 that the Common Market came into being. Not to be overlooked is the fact that the treaty was *signed in Rome*. It sought to bring about economic oneness and political unity. Some of the countries which join the Common Market may later seek to withdraw. Others will probably seek to be admitted. But if this European effort succeeds (and there is every reason to believe that it will) we should not be surprised to find the events of Daniel and Revelation coming to pass very soon. We must remember, however, that the translation of the Church must take place first. And since that is so, there is good cause to prepare ourselves for the lift-off at any moment.

As is the case with the United Nations, so it is with the Common Market. We are not branding it all bad. It is probably a necessity for the survival of the many small countries of Europe faced with the pressure of Communistic aggression. What we are saying is that it appears to be laying the foundation for the oppressive economic controls held in the hands of ten nations under the direct veto power of a universal dictator. Mention was made of nations wanting to withdraw. And it is not outside the realm of possibility that this may be what is meant in Daniel's vision of "three of the first horns [rulers in the confederacy] plucked up by the roots" (Daniel 7:8). These may be nations in the new Roman Empire who see the direction in which the whole thing is moving during the days after the translation of the Church. They may rebel against the policy of the Antichrist. If they do, they will simply be "plucked up" or annihilated.

A Realized Religious Ecumenism

In His high priestly prayer our Lord prayed, "That they all may be one; as thou, Father, art in me, and I in thee, that they also may be one in us . . ." (John 17:21). Within the last half-century there has been a growing stampede to bring all Christian bodies together in a monolithic structure under the auspices of the World Council of Churches. It is held by many ecclesiastical leaders that in doing so the prayer of Jesus will be answered. One thing usually overlooked is the fact that it is God in His sovereign power who creates unity, not man in his weak and fallen nature. No amount of frenzied effort on man's part to thin doctrinal positions to a watery kind of spiritual bouillon will bring about the oneness for which Jesus prayed. In fact, structural union has little to do with Christian unity. Structural union may be achieved (at least between the consenting larger denominations within a few years), but it will be based on a theological premise so frail as to make questionable its continued identification as the "Body of Christ."

History records a time when there was only one Church. For a thousand years no one dared to break away from the sacrosanct institution. Then men in the East decided to sever the tie and launch out on their own. Less than five hundred years later came the biggest split of all—the Protestant Reformation. All of us know what kind of "oneness" existed prior to the days of Martin Luther. It was union in the darkness of spiritual sterility. Apostasy was another name for the Church. Not until Luther braved the storm did anyone enter into a head-on collision with the most powerful and domineering organization in the world— the Roman Catholic church. Some insist today that the Reformation was a mistake—at least far too drastic—and that the Christian community must return to a oneness similar to that which characterized the Church before the sixteenth century.

We should expect to see stronger measures being taken against the local churches and independent groups who resist the ecumenical design of the World Council. But eventually there will be one World Church. If not before, certainly during the period after the lift-off of the Bride of Christ there will be only one organizational structure of religion. A full description of this superchurch is found in the Apocalypse (Revelation 16, 17) where the post lift-off Church is called "a woman [sitting] upon a scarlet coloured beast" and "MYSTERY, BABYLON THE GREAT, THE MOTHER OF HARLOTS AND ABOMINATIONS OF THE EARTH." Before the close of the final week of prophecy (Daniel's seventieth week) this World Church will be destroyed by the Antichrist and he will set himself up as God in the Temple on Mount Zion. Paul refers to this in one of his many letters. Of the end-time ruler he writes,

> Who opposeth and exalteth himself above all that is called God, or that is worshipped; so that he as God sitteth in the temple of God, shewing himself that he is God.
>
> 2 Thessalonians 2:4; cf. Revelation 17:16

All this is in keeping with the restoration of the Roman Empire in which Caesar worship was obligatory. The old paganism will be back in greater force than ever in the past. The one-government, one-economy, one-church world will finally be a reality and the proud dreams of a God-denying, Christ-ignoring people shall come true.

Peace and War

The first half of the final week on the prophetic calendar will be a period of peace and prosperity. This will be in the interest of the Antichrist's phenomenal rise to power. We are not told precisely how soon after the translation of the Church this world ruler will be acclaimed by *every* nation as supreme dictator. It may not be until near the middle of the week. But wonders shall not cease as men convince themselves that the Kingdom of Heaven has arrived under the divine powers displayed by the beast with the "iron teeth" (Daniel 7:7) and "feet part of iron and part of clay" (2:33). At first the Antichrist shall not be supreme ruler except over the strongest confederacy of nations in the revived Roman Empire. Some "barbarians" will still be outside and, though enamored with the bestial dictator to the point of full cooperation, will later create much trouble for his planned kingdom of peaceful submission. These events will be treated with careful attention at a later point in our discussion.

It is the latter half of the seven years which will issue in terrible conflict between nations such as has never been witnessed. Not even our wildest dreams of a nuclear war can begin to conjure an image of man's death and desolation as horrifying as that which will then take place. Men will cry, ". . . Peace, peace; when there is no peace" (Jeremiah 6:14) for "when they shall say, Peace and safety; then sudden destruction cometh upon them, as travail upon a woman with child; and they shall not escape" (1 Thessalonians 5:3).

To realize peace is not enough. Any absence of war which is constructed on man's ingenious devising is disappointing. Never in history has it been any different. Only during the time of Jesus' earthly life was there peace all over the world for any length of time. Unredeemed men cannot keep their treaties long without growing restless. Christ is the Prince of Peace and no lasting peace will be effected until His millennial reign. For this reason He Himself predicted that there shall be "wars and rumors of wars" (Matthew 24:6). While it is true that the Master is here dealing with conditions during the last prophetic week, we may be certain that the prophecy is also apropos to this prelift-off period of deepening apostasy and self-sufficiency. If we would only recognize this basic point we would see our peace efforts in a new light. Anyone with eyes and ears knows full well that the modern world is a tinderbox and becoming more explosive each year. The situation is certainly not getting better (as some churchmen have sought to make us believe) but worse and worse as Jesus and His disciples warned long ago.

6
A Red Carpet for the Messiah!

An Appearance of Safety

While the true Church is enjoying the marriage supper of the Lamb and rejoicing in the rewards given them in heaven at the "judgment seat of Christ" (2 Corinthians 5:8–11), the masses left on the earth will be exulting in the hope of an earthly redeemer of the whole world. The Jews in the nation of Israel will be beside themselves with rapturous joy in the belief that their long-awaited Messiah has appeared at last. This prominent political figure (who has been becoming more and more popular in the years just prior to the disappearance of the Church) will be looking suspiciously like the kind of man destined to rule the earth. There is good reason to believe that Antichrist will be engaged in world affairs previous to lift-off, maybe even now known to millions of people as just another government statesman.

> Let no man deceive you by any means: for that day shall not come, except there come a falling away first, and that man of sin be revealed, the son of perdition.
>
> 2 Thessalonians 2:3

The apostasy, to which Paul directs our attention in these words, is obviously far advanced at the present time.

Since he will be received as the deliverer long-awaited by the Jewish people, this exciting personality will most likely be of Jewish extraction —at least someone from the general area of the Middle East. It must not be overlooked, however, that this false Messiah might be of Arabic extraction. The Arabic peoples are descendants of Abraham by Hagar and, although not among the chosen people themselves, are destined to be an irritation to the Hebrews. Following the birth of Ishmael (father of the Arabs) God said to Abraham, ". . . a father of many nations have I made thee . . . and kings shall come out of thee" (Genesis 17:5, 6). It is not at all incredible to foresee the age-old conflict between the kings of the Arabic peoples and the kings of the Israelites brought to a climax in a final struggle between the son of the slave woman (anti-Messiah) and the son of Sarah (the true Messiah). At this point, of course, we are only speculating as to who this false Messiah may turn out to be.

So successful will he be in settling international disputes that the Gentiles will be determined to yield their most exalted seats of power to him. And so beautifully will he handle the Arab-Israeli powder keg that the Jews will know that the heir to David's throne has come.

His words will be smooth, his appearance regal, his bearing like that of a god, and his diplomacy unequalled by mortal man. With the conflict surrounding Israel seemingly ended, the Jewish nation will thank their God for the peace and security of the restored Kingdom. Almost anything suggested by the redeemer of the Jews will be readily accepted. And this in spite of Jesus' stern warning, "I am come in my Father's name, and ye receive me not: if another shall come in his own name, him ye will receive" (John 5:43). Of course, at this time the Hebrew nation will still be a victim of unbelief in their Messiah who came to earth and was rejected by them long ago.

The New Covenant

Jeremiah foresaw the glad day (after God has finished with His chastisement of the people of Abraham) when there would be a new relationship between the Lord and the persecuted *diaspora* (scattered nation). He calls it "a new covenant," a relationship with God which will be far superior to the one broken by the wandering Hebrews while Moses was on the mount and later reflected in their Lawgiver's symbolic act in which he smashed the rock on which were inscribed the Decalogue or Ten Commandments (Exodus 32:1–20). This covenant would be written on the heart rather than on slabs of stone. It is well for us to hear the prophet's own words,

Behold, the days are coming, says the Lord, when I will make a new covenant with the house of Israel and the house of Judah, not like the covenant which I made with their fathers when I took them by the hand to bring them out of the land of Egypt, my covenant which they broke, though I was their husband, says the Lord. But this is the covenant which I will make with the house of Israel after those days, says the Lord: I will put my law within them, and I will write it upon their hearts; and I will be their God, and they shall be my people. And no longer shall each man teach his neighbor and each his brother, saying, "Know the Lord," for they shall all know me, from the least of them to the greatest, says the Lord; for I will forgive their iniquity and I will remember their sin no more.

Jeremiah 31:31–34 RSV

When the Antichrist (false Messiah) has expanded his power and prestige to the point where the Roman Empire will install him as the new Caesar, one of his first acts will be to draw up a treaty with the Hebrew nation. Daniel calls this treaty "a strong covenant." Apparently, he will have been so overwhelming in his success in terminating the Middle-East conflict that all parties will agree to the treaty. With his own signature on the covenant the governing puppets of Israel will have every reason to trust its validity and permanence. No more prestigious and forceful person in the world could be found to put his name on a treaty. Daniel describes the actual ratification of the treaty in these words,

And he shall make a strong covenant with many for one week; and for half of the week he shall cause sacrifice and offering to cease, and upon the wing of abominations shall come one who makes desolate, until the decreed end is poured out on the desolator.

Daniel 9:27 RSV

This covenant shall assure the Jews of protection against any and all aggression and the nation of Israel, still blinded in disbelief, will think of the arrangement as the fulfillment of Jeremiah's prophecy. Thus their plight will be worsened in their failure to see how the world is being duped.

New Messiah's Identity Revealed

At the time of the ratification of a treaty between Israel and the Roman Empire, the end-time Caesar will reveal his true identity. This must not be construed to mean that the malicious nature, later to become prominent in his reign, is to become recognizable at this time. On the contrary, the shrewd dictator's pattern will be to create an image of brotherly love and kindness. He will even talk piously about God and his respect for Him. Through such deceitful tactics, however, his person will gradually develop the kind of holy aura which would induce people to see him as more than a man. Something mysterious will pervade his person and wherever he goes men will praise and adore him. At the signing of the treaty will be as good a place as any for this demonic ruler to accept the opinions of the masses and announce himself as their Messiah.

Palms will wave again in the city of Jerusalem and men will cry in great accolades of Messianic praise, "Hosanna! Hosanna! Hosanna to him who comes in the name of the Lord! Hosanna in the highest!" At last, David will have returned to bring peace and prosperity to Israel forever. Celebrations will be held across the land and all the nations of the Roman Empire will send their greetings and congratulations. What a day it shall be. From every mouth in the Land of Promise will rise the shout, "The King is here! Our Kingdom is reborn!"

Lest there be any doubt in the minds of any, immediate orders will be issued for the rebuilding of the Temple of David on Mount Zion. The fact that the Dome of the Rock is now located there and is controlled by the Muslims of the Arabic world creates no problem. With the Arab-Israeli conflict settled and the fresh smell of peace in the air, not even the Muslims will object to this move. After all, everything will be moving toward one worldwide religion based solely on the Fatherhood of God and the brotherhood of man. We are already well on our way to making this the only foundation for a religious syncretism including all types of otherwise incompatible beliefs. It is possible that the suave ruler will convince all people that the only way to insure peace is through a unified religion which would bind the empire together. That is exactly the tactic used by the Caesars in the early days of Christianity. And if this is the plan, Antichrist will capitalize on the universal Father-hood-brotherhood concept.

The Jews will have a great thing going for them at the beginning of the last week in Daniel's prophecy. Theirs will be control of one of the richest countries in the world—rich in possessions and in tradition. After two thousand years their land will be restored, their wandering people at peace, and their Temple rebuilt. What is even more fantastic to contemplate, their Messiah will have come and it cannot be long until he establishes the throne of David again at Jerusalem. Everything will be in readiness for that glorious moment prayed for by wailing Hebrews for many centuries. We may project a frenzied situation in which the wealthy government of Israel will begin building a palace for their Messiah the moment he signs the treaty.

Sacrifices Reinstated

Once the Temple is erected on that holy mount, the system of sacrifices shall be given rebirth with bloody offerings on the altar as in the days before the Temple of Herod was demolished in A.D. 70. The whole ritual will be revived and priests will be plentiful in the land. No more will wailing be heard at the ancient wall of tears for there will be nothing to wail about. Passover feasts will still hold a high place in the Jewish year, but a new festival of *Regathering* will be instituted to mark the restoration of the land and the rebuilding of the Temple.

Lambs, bullocks, and turtledoves shall abound in great numbers. No one will be so poor that he cannot provide himself with a victim of sacrifice without blemish. The welcome smell of blood in the holy precincts shall be like perfume to families so long forbidden the actual blessing of temple sacrifice. Jews who do not dwell in the rejuvenated kingdom at the first will again make their annual pilgrimages to the holy mount to share in the observance of Passover and *Regathering.*

Ironic as it may be, the whole reinstated system of sacrifices is an example of traditional redundancy. Though Christ has put an end to the need for such offerings by the sacrifice of Himself on the cross, the unbelieving Jews at the outset of the final week will not yet be conscious of this truth known to the Church for the past nineteen hundred years as a *mystery* of divine grace. Therefore, the gory details of an arrangement instituted by God as a temporary measure until the perfect sacrifice was given will be repetitiously pursued. The whole scene will be like men desperately seeking the assurance of divine acceptance without ever coming to the knowledge that it is done.

Absence of the Restrainer

Let us reiterate that none of the above events can take place until the Church is gone. With the departure of the Church from the earth is also the removal of the Holy Spirit. Assuredly, the Spirit of God will always be in His world in limited fashion even during the last prophetic week. That Spirit was on earth, though faintly, during the days before the Flood. In the same way the Third Person of the Trinity will be here during the days preceding the coming judgment in fire. But the mighty working power which came to the Church on the day of Pentecost will be withdrawn so as to allow the will of unregenerate man to show itself at its very worst.

The Apostle Paul is specific about this in the Second Thessalonian letter. He has just been clarifying the minds of his friends in relation to the rise of Antichrist which, he insists, cannot happen as long as the Holy Spirit is in the world.

> You know what is restraining him [Antichrist] now so that he may be revealed in his time. For the mystery of lawlessness is already at work, only he [Holy Spirit] who now restrains it will do so until he [Holy Spirit] is out of the way. And then the lawless one will be revealed. . . .
>
> 2 Thessalonians 2:6–8

A definite relationship exists between Christ and the Church as well as between the Holy Spirit and the Church. The Church is the "Body of

Christ" which means that the removal of the Christian community is a withdrawal of the *whole* Christ from the earth since the Head of the Body is with the Father even now. The author of Hebrews puts it well, ". . . Christ is not entered into the holy places made with hands . . . but into heaven itself, now to appear in the presence of God for us" (Hebrews 9:24). Likewise, the "Body of Christ" is the temple of the Holy Spirit which was initially indwelt at Pentecost. Thus, when the Church is gone, both Christ and the Holy Spirit are no longer present on the earth.

An interesting and illuminating observation is to be noted in the extensive account of the last prophetic week in the Book of Revelation (chapters 6–19). Not once is the New Testament word for Church *(ecclesia)* used by the apocalyptic narrator. This must be because there was no true Church seen by John on the earth to be involved in this period of trouble. Likewise, while the Spirit is present in the second and third chapters (when the Church is still in the world—Revelation 2:7, 11, 17, 29; 3:6, 13, 22), and in the last chapter (which portrays the heavenly sphere in the life to come—22:17), He is conspicuously absent in the intervening chapters which depict the last week of trouble. When the Church is lifted off the earth to meet the Lord in the air, so also does the Spirit depart in His office of enduement and reinforcement reserved for the *ecclesia.* At that moment, Satan is free to present his Messianic substitute to the world.

The Satanic Imitation of the Trinity

Satan is behind the total program scheduled for the last week in the calendar of prophecy. As his position becomes stronger (with Christ, the Holy Spirit, and the Church out of the way), the desperate adversary of man and the hater of God will no longer hide anything. For everything God does, the devil has a counterfeit. The most devilish scheme of all his deceptions is his attempt to foist on the world an unholy trinity as an imitation of the Holy Trinity of God. Satan himself will serve in the capacity of God the Father and men will be so duped and blinded by their unbelief that they will not be capable of telling the difference. John calls him the *Dragon,* reminiscent of the *Serpent* in the Creation story

(Genesis 3:1), as well as *Satan* and *Devil* (Revelation 12:9, 20:2). During this time God will have withdrawn from the world of men to let man run things in his own damning way until the time of judgment arrives. Under such conditions, Satan will have complete freedom to act the part of God and create a hell on earth.

The Second Person of the Trinity, our Lord Jesus Christ, will be counterfeited by the Antichrist called the *lawless one* (2 Thessalonians 2:8 RSV), the *man of sin* and *son of perdition* (2 Thessalonians 2:3), and the *beast* (Daniel 7:7; Revelation 13:1; 19:20). He will be everything that Christ was not—evil, selfish, deceptive, and destructive. Yet, he will claim deity and perform many wondrous signs to dazzle the populace. The wonders are probably to be a combination of scientific wizardry and demonic power. His greatest feat is predicted to be some kind of fake resurrection by which he comes back to life after a mortal wound has been inflicted on his person (13:3). Whether this will be a resuscitation from what appeared to be death but was not, or an amazing demonstration of a yet-to-be-discovered scientific marvel, we do not know. Whatever it is that happens we may be sure that it will be effected by the direct power of Satan who has access to the world of evil spirits. The purpose will be to mimic the death and resurrection of Jesus and thus annul the work of God once and for all. And the people will be so overwhelmed by this spectacle as to fall down and worship him.

If Christ has a substitute during these troubled times, so will the Holy Spirit. The Apocalypse makes reference to "the false prophet" (19:20), also called "another beast" (13:11–17), who serves as the dictator's assistant. There can be little doubt that this man is the head of the ecclesiastical organization represented by the "Mother of Harlots" (17:5) which is later destroyed by the Antichrist. Since the false prophet is still around at the judgment of the beast, we may assume that the religious head of the superchurch is kept around to serve the cause of the satanic ruler after the annihilation of his institution and liquidation of the clergy. It will be the responsibility of this false prophet to draw attention to the Antichrist, not to himself (13:12). Immediately one notes the similarity between the work of the Holy Spirit in relation to Christ and that of the false prophet in relation to the Beast.

> When the Spirit of truth comes, he will guide you into all truth;
> for he will not speak on his own authority . . . He will glorify me,
> for he will take what is mine and declare it to you.
>
> John 16:13, 14 RSV

Clearly seen is the plot of deception and destruction laid out by the enemy of God. All God's works will be counterfeited. Replacing the Trinity of Father, Son and Holy Spirit will be the Antitrinity of Satan, Antichrist, and the false prophet. The Beast and his lying prophet will work as a team to carry out the will of their father. If Jesus said to the Pharisees, "Ye are of your father the devil . . ." (John 8:44), how much more shall those words be true of the godless pair who do the will of Satan in the end of the age!

Israel Attacked from the North

About six hundred years before the coming of Christ as a babe in Bethlehem, the prophet Ezekiel envisioned a time following the restoration of Israel as a nation (Ezekiel 37:21–23) when the Land of Promise would be invaded by an armed force from the north country (38, 39). Only one people live due north of the little state of Israel and that is the mammoth Union of Soviet Socialist Republics known as Russia. A hair-raising fact is found in studying any modern map. The city of Moscow, capital of Russia, is *directly north* of the city of Jerusalem! It is as though the two cities—satanic and divine—stand ready for the final conflict.

A number of strange-sounding place names describing specific areas in the north are employed by the prophet at a time when the Scythians were in control of the area. No such names were employed by these nomadic peoples nor had anyone heard of places by these names anywhere in the world. After six hundred years in this vast northern world the Scythians were replaced by the Sarmatians in the third century before Christ. Still no words like those used by Ezekiel. Later came the Goths, Huns, Avars, Khazars, and Eastern Bulgars. But none of these hordes of people used the prophet's names. Then, in the ninth century after Christ, appeared the Eastern Slavs, ancestors of the modern Russians. The founding of the Russian state is credited to Rurik who settled in Novgorod in A.D. 862. It was after this time that the names of modern Russia began to appear.

What are those place-names referred to by Ezekiel fifteen hundred years before they were used? Let the prophet speak in his own words,

> The word of Jehovah came unto me saying, Son of man, set thy face toward Gog of the land of Magog, the prince of Rosh, Meshech, and Tubal, and prophesy against him, and say, Thus saith the Lord Jehovah: Behold, I am against thee, O Gog, prince of Rosh, Meshech, and Tubal. . . . Persia, Cush, and Put with them . . . Gomer and all his hordes; the house of Togarmah in the uttermost parts of the north, and all his hordes, even many people with thee.
>
> Ezekiel 38:1–6 ASV

It is concluded by biblical historians (as well as secular) and geographers that *Gog* and *Magog* refer to the far north of Russia in the area of the Caucasus mountains which still go by the name *Gogh*. When the modern term *Russia* is rendered in Hebrew it is the exact word used by Ezekiel and translated into English as *Rosh*. *Moscow* is the modern rendering of *Meshech*, the name of an early fighting tribe, and *Tobolsk* is named for the offspring of the northern people of *Tubal*. *Cush* is Ethiopia, *Put* or *Phut* is Libya, and *Gomer* is Germany. *Togarmah* was the son of the ancient tribal father, *Gomer*, and the name was preserved in the Eastern Cappodocian city of *Til-garimmu* referred to in the records of Assyria. Thus, most of the words are place names in Russia today. (For general information on all these names see S. Maxwell Coder's "The Future of Russia" in *Focus on Prophecy*, edited by Charles L. Feinberg, pages 81-83; also see Clarence E. Mason, Jr.'s "Gog and Magog, Who and Where" in *Prophecy in the Seventies*, also edited by Feinberg, pages 221–226.)

The fact that Germany is mentioned as a northern ally is interesting in the light of Soviet domination of East Germany. The remaining peoples of the Arabic world are Ethiopia, Libya, and Persia. While the powerful leadership will come from Russia in the invasion of Israel, there will be a confederacy of the north country which will include soldiers from these Israeli-hating allies. As the Russians move down on the Land of Promise they will be supported by an upward surge from Africa as well as a generous smattering of troops from Iran (Persia). Daniel suggests that the north country will deceitfully turn on the south and the Libyans and Ethiopians shall be crushed (Daniel 11:40–45). This would be typical of the past history of Russian alliances since the Bolshevik Revolution in 1917.

Russia will invade Palestine because of the vast riches in this coveted valley of the world. At the bottom of the Dead Sea alone are mineral deposits which will make the rest of the world look like a pauper planet. Any nation who can claim these riches and bring them up from the floor of the salty sea will command the lead in the world's economy. This is His land and it is still the richest little parcel of earth in the world. (For more information on this untapped wealth read Harry Rimmer's *The Coming War and Rise of Russia* and Hal Lindsey's *The Late Great Planet Earth.*) Later during the final week of prophecy, the Roman Empire will decide to ravish Israel for the same reason. It will be noted that the Antichrist and his revived empire will not be involved in this particular invasion. The pact between Russia and the Arab League in our time only adds to the certainty of this attack exactly as Ezekiel prophesied twenty-five hundred years ago.

The war will be the shortest in history and will end in the most devastating defeat in the annals of war. No sooner than Russia arrives in the Land of Promise, the Lord will utterly demolish the weapons and crush the troops. Ezekiel tells it as he saw it:

> . . . in that day there shall be a great shaking in the land of Israel.
> . . . Behold, I am against thee, O Gog, prince of Rosh, Meshech, and Tubal. . . . I will smite thy bow out of thy left hand, and will cause thine arrows to fall out of thy right hand. Thou shalt fall upon the mountains of Israel, thou, and all thy hordes, and the peoples that are with thee: I will give thee unto the ravenous birds of every sort, and to the beasts of the field to be devoured. . . . And I will send a fire on Magog, and on them that dwell securely in the isles; and they shall know that I am Jehovah. And my holy name will I

make known in the midst of my people Israel; neither will I suffer my holy name to be profaned anymore: and the nations shall know that I am Jehovah, the Holy One in Israel.

Ezekiel 38:19; 39:1, 3–7 ASV.

This divine intervention on behalf of the Jewish people will render the nation of Russia crippled beyond the point of ever being a contender against the Roman Empire. In fact, this crushing defeat will probably force the north country into total submission to the Antichrist's growing power. Most likely, this invasion will take place in the first half of the last prophetic week. In fact, it is probably scheduled for the early days of the post lift-off period since the entire last week lasts only seven years and Ezekiel states that it will take that long to clean up the weapons and burn them (39:9, 10). It is significant to note that the Dutch people have invented a new kind of material called *Lignostone* which the Russians are now utilizing in their weapons of war. It is extremely strong but it burns with a fierce fire! So terrible will be the devastation of Russian troops that "seven months shall the house of Israel be burying of them . . ." (39:12).

The Effect on Overpopulation

Communism is the worst anti-God scourge in the modern world. Many have feared, in view of the godless and ruthless reign of terror coming out of Russia, that atheistic communism will one day rule the world. Not a chance! It is fitting that this smashing defeat should come to God's longstanding enemy and that it should be meted out by the very God whom Russia has defied. The whole communistic threat will continue until that day when God says it is enough. Then, in a blinding flash of judgment, it will be all over.

Not all the Russians will be annihilated in the invasion. A small remnant of them will be spared to participate with the rest of the world in the Battle of Armageddon. The prophet is rather exact in his estimate of the horrible massacre: "I will turn thee back, and leave but the sixth part of thee . . ." (39:2). (The Revised Standard Version omits the reference to a *sixth part* as do several translations. Many scholars feel that this verse does not allow the King James rendering but actually insists on the total destruction of Russia.)

The population of Russia today is about 250 million. By the year 2000 it will be about 360 million. (This is the mean figure between the low and high variables as given by Ehrlich in *Population, Resources, Environment*, pages 337–340.) If the satellites of Russia located in the north country should be included, the number of people multiplies exceedingly. The reference, however, is specifically to Gog, Rosh, Meshech, and Tubal which is the country of Russia only. On the basis of the projected population at the end of the present millennium, five-sixths of the Russian people will approximate three hundred million people! One can immediately see that this is another step in the solution to the population explosion. "This is the Lord's doing, it is marvellous in our eyes" (Psalms 118:23; *see also* Mark 12:11).

Of interest is the fact that Joel and John both symbolize these times of judgment as an act of divine *reaping*. In his vision of the multitudes in the valley of decision at the end of the age, Joel hears God saying, "Put in the sickle, for the harvest is ripe . . ." (Joel 3:13 RSV). John later sees the fulfillment of the prophet's words in the end-time of history when Christ is seated on a white cloud with a sharp sickle in His hand. Suddenly, an angel is heard addressing Him who sits on the cloud, "Put in your sickle, and reap, for the hour to reap has come, for the harvest of the earth is fully ripe" (Revelation 14:15 RSV). Perhaps there is a prophetic insight even in the use of the word *sickle* since the most godless peoples of these last days are living under that very sign. The symbol of communism is the sickle on a red flag. This may be God's way of saying that the greatest sign of atheism shall be turned into an instrument of divine destruction.

The Times Seem out of Joint

Long before the creation of man, Satan had been expelled from the place of brightness and power with God which had formerly been his. With the successful seduction of man, this archenemy of the Creator usurped the control of the earth which had been intended for Adam. Thus Satan became "the god of this world" (2 Corinthians 4:4). This does not imply that he was no longer permitted in the presence of the Lord. Job makes this clear at the outset of his drama of human suffering: "Now there was a day when the sons of God came to present themselves before the Lord, and Satan also came among them" (Job 1:6). Neither does his being "the god of this world" mean that Satan has been limited to man's earth. What this actually says is that the enemy of God and the tempter of man has access to the world for purposes of seduction and access to the dwelling place of God for the accusation of Adam's offspring.

Quite clearly the New Testament places the headquarters of Satan and his demonic forces in the atmospheric heavens. In a figurative sense, his dwelling place is between God and man. Paul calls him "the prince of the power of the air" (Ephesians 2:2). John sees him being permanently excommunicated from both the abode of God and the atmospheric heavens in the latter days.

> And the great dragon was thrown down, that ancient serpent, who is called the Devil and Satan, the deceiver of the whole world —he was thrown down to the earth, and his angels were thrown down with him. . . . woe to you, O earth and sea, for the devil has come down to you in great wrath, because he knows that his time is short!
>
> Revelation 12:9, 12 RSV

With the translation of the Church and the withdrawal of the Holy Spirit, Satan will make his grand entrance into the world where all his forces will be loosed upon mankind. To the Church, Paul says, ". . . we are . . . contending against spiritual hosts of wickedness in the heavenly places" (Ephesians 6:12 RSV), but once the Church is gone, the arena of demonic operation will be the earth itself. Nothing will restrain the intents of Satan except in rare exceptions to be investigated later.

Naturally, with this kind of situation prevailing one would be bound to expect the times to be out of joint. It is in light of this truth that we begin to understand what is implied in the seven seals, seven trumpets, and seven vials of the Apocalypse (6–16). One horrible disaster follows on the heels of the one preceding it and each succeeding one gets worse.

Not only man is affected but the beasts, fowl, fish, trees, vegetation, and water feel the terrible result of man's disobedience. The first seal (6:1, 2) reveals the arrival of Antichrist who pretends to bring peace by carrying a bow with no arrow, but who is bent on conquering all mankind.

At once, under the second seal, war appears in the wake of the false Christ. This is probably a reference to the invasion of Israel by Russia discussed above. Of course, this seal must represent the many "wars and rumors of wars" during this period. In any event, the revelation under each seal gets worse until the seventh which is so bad that the seven trumpeters have to announce it in stages. Likewise, the messages of the trumpeters grow more terrible until the last one which is divided into seven vials of wrath poured on the earth. And so conditions on the earth grow progressively more intolerable, so unbearable that the duped Jews and Gentiles both are in for an unbelievable disaster.

7
In the Middle of the Week

Israel Is Betrayed

In Daniel's prophecy of the seventy weeks (Daniel 9:24–27) the last week, which is the time of the Antichrist, is said to be divided in the middle by a crucial development. The events described in the preceding chapter are believed by the writer to take place during the first half of the prophetic week, that is, during the first three and one-half years. An exception must be made for the seals, trumpets, and vials which range across the total week.

One cannot begin to comprehend the Book of Revelation without a good grasp of the contents of the Old Testament Book of Daniel. The key for interpretation of the Apocalypse is found in the prophecies of one who saw the mysteries of the Lord nearly seven hundred years before the last book of the New Testament was written. In Revelation one encounters such expressions as "one thousand two-hundred and sixty days" (Revelation 11:3; 12:6 RSV) and "forty-two months" (11:2; 13:5 RSV). These periods of time add up to three and one-half years in each case. Furthermore, the strange expression "time, and times, and half a time" is found in this vision of the Apostle John (12:14). Obviously, we have the same period of time referred to here under a different analogy: "one year, plus two years, plus one-half year" equals three and one half years. How do we know that this is the meaning of these prophetic calculations? Our clue is in the Book of Daniel.

In the closing chapter of his prophecy, Daniel tells of hearing a "man clothed in linen" (clearly a divine being) inform him of the duration of the troubles which he has just seen. The spokesman says that "it would be for a time, two times, and half a time; and that when the shattering of the power of the holy people comes to an end all these things would be accomplished" (Daniel 12:7 RSV). In the earlier passage to which we have often referred, the prophet writes of the last prophetic week,

> And he shall make a firm covenant with many for one week: and in the midst of the week he shall cause the sacrifice and the oblation to cease and upon the wing of abominations shall come one that maketh desolate; and even unto the full end, and that determined, shall wrath be poured out upon the desolate.
>
> Daniel 9:27 ASV

The week is seven years in length, as determined from the context and its fulfillment in history, and it is divided in the middle. Half of seven is three and one-half years.

From all this, it is apparent that something of tremendous consequence is going to transpire. It will happen in the middle of the coming seven years of satanic reign. Daniel says that the covenant made between the pagan prince and the restored nation of Israel will be broken, sacrifices stopped, and "the abomination that maketh desolate" (12:11) will be set up. In 168 B.C. Antiochus Epiphanes stopped the daily sacrifices in the Temple and built a brazen altar of an idolatrous image at which sacrifices were made to Jupiter Olympius (1 Maccabee 1: 54; 6:7; 2 Maccabee 6:2). Many zealous Jews were sure that Daniel's prophecy had been fulfilled when they saw the Greek abomination of the holy place. Two centuries later Jesus declared that this was not so. The abomination of desolation was yet to come and He warned His Jewish brethren about it.

> So when you see the desolating sacrilege spoken of by the prophet Daniel, standing in the holy place (let the reader understand), then let those who are in Judea flee to the mountains; let him who is on the housetop not go down to take what is in his house; and let him who is in the field not turn back to take his mantle. . . . For then there will be great tribulation, such as has not been from the beginning of the world until now, no, and never will be.
>
> Matthew 24:15–18, 21 RSV (*See also* Mark 13:14.)

The events recorded in Matthew 24 and Mark 13 are all reserved for this calamitous period at the end of the age predicted by Daniel and John. When the sixth century prophet, the first century apostle, and Jesus are brought together on this matter we discover that the story is terrifying to anticipate but simple to interpret. The Beast (Antichrist), who at the beginning of the final week ratifies a treaty of peace with the Jews and assists in rebuilding their Temple, will betray the nation of Israel. In the middle of the week (after three and one-half years) he will break his covenant, desecrate the Temple, and put an end to the Jewish system of sacrifices.

Antichrist Sits on Mount Zion

The middle of the week will be the beginning of "Jacob's trouble" (Jeremiah 30:4–7). Incredible as it may seem to them, the beneficent dictator of the revived Roman Empire will turn into a vicious, murderous, insane persecutor of millions of Jews who had become convinced that he was the long-awaited Messiah. After waiting two thousand years for the restoration of the nation of Israel, the people of Abraham will have occupied their Temple only two or three years when they are suddenly forced into pagan captivity again—this time in their own land!

Antichrist will be strong enough by the middle of the week to announce himself dictator of the whole world, not just of the Roman Empire. Where else could he find a more appropriate location for his capital than Jerusalem? And where in the whole world could a higher throne be found than the one in the Temple where only God is supposed to sit? Jews, Christians, and Muslims all consider that holy mount as sacred. The psychological conditioning of the minds of the masses would be electrifying.

Once he has entered the Temple and usurped the Holy of Holies for himself, the Antichrist will declare his self-inflated identity to the world over which he rules. Enamored by amazing feats of scientific and satanic power, the masses of subjects in the Gentile world will gladly accept the pseudodeity of the Beast. The prophet, on whom we have been most dependent for our insight into this closing-out of the present world order, writes,

. . . he shall exalt himself and magnify himself above every god, and shall speak astonishing things against the God of gods. He shall prosper till the indignation is accomplished; for what is determined shall be done. He shall give no heed to the gods of his fathers, or to the one beloved by women; he shall not give heed to any other god, for he shall magnify himself above all.

                                                        Daniel 11:36, 37 RSV

Paul predicts the same action on the part of "the man of lawlessness . . . the son of perdition, who opposes and exalts himself against every so-called god or object of worship, so that he takes his seat in the temple of God, proclaiming himself to be God" (2 Thessalonians 2:3, 4 RSV).

Such a disgusting development of blasphemy could never happen if it were not for the obstinate rebellion and disbelief of the nation of Israel. Throughout their long history, the Abrahamic people have suffered untold anguish because they have miserably failed to live up to the great covenant given to them by God four thousand years ago. Captivity and dispersion have not succeeded in bringing them to an acceptance of the Messiah. Only scattered instances of Jewish conversion have been recorded through the centuries. Moses warned the nation that its favored position under God would not last unless the people were faithful to the covenant made at Sinai. The consequences of disobedience would be found in their becoming "the tail" rather than the head (Deuteronomy 28:13, 44). Nowhere does God say that He will annul the covenant, but He does warn that the result of disbelief and disobedience will be severe chastisement. The punishment continues until this day and will be culminated during the last prophetic week as the natural end of rejecting Christ and accepting Antichrist.

A Remnant Sealed in Israel

The Remnant which God preserved in Babylon has grown to over twelve million Jews in today's world. And this in spite of the fact that multiplied numbers of these chosen people have been murdered by anti-Semites throughout the intervening years. It has been impossible to eradicate the sturdy stock of Abraham. Hitler was sure that he had found "a solution to the Jewish problem" in killing six million of them in five years, but he could not have been more in error in his judgment. Most of the twelve million contemporary Hebrews will be finally absorbed into the rapidly-growing population of the new Israeli state.

If there is any one thing made crystal clear in the prophecies, it is that the largest percentage of these returning descendants of Abraham will rebuild their nation in disbelief. Their Messiah will still be rejected and, in His place, they will accept the pseudo-Messiah as Lord and Saviour. In the midst of the seven years of trouble the Lord will deliberately raise up a cadre of Jewish witnesses who will announce the coming of the true Kingdom. This will be the Remnant chosen by Jehovah out of the massive number of descendants of Abraham who have multiplied over the centuries. Actually, what we have here is a Remnant of the remnant! John numbers them at one hundred forty-four thousand.

> After this I saw four angels standing at the four corners of the earth, holding the four winds of the earth, that no wind should blow on the earth, or on the sea, or upon any tree. And I saw another angel ascend from the sunrising, having the seal of the living God: and he cried with a great voice to the four angels to whom it was given to hurt the earth and the sea, saying, Hurt not the earth, neither the sea, nor the trees, till we shall have sealed the servants of our God on their foreheads. And I heard the number of them that were sealed, a hundred and forty-four thousand, sealed out of every tribe of the children of Israel. . . .
>
> Revelation 7:1–4 ASV

In the following verses, John lists the twelve tribes by name and divides the total number of sealed witnesses into equal parts of twelve thousand for each tribe. There is no reason not to accept this careful divine numbering as literal. The argument of some that none are of the true Jews except the descendants of Judah must be carefully weighed. God finds faithful witnesses in each of the tribes. And though ten tribes were lost in the Assyrian captivity, they were not lost to God who knows where every child of Abraham is at every moment. These witnesses will probably see clearly what is happening in Israel as the power of Antichrist increases.

By the middle of the time of trouble, these responsive Jews will have decided that the acclaimed Messiah is a counterfeit. Small groups will begin to secretly form out of which will come the complete number of one hundred forty-four thousand. God will send His angel to *seal* these men prior to the godless seal which the Beast will enforce for all people. That is, the Lord will beat the Beast to these select Jews and brand them as His own. The seal will be on their foreheads, which is where the Beast will later put his mark. But on these one hundred forty-four thousand the mark of blasphemy will not take. They will be preserved from death throughout "the time of Jacob's trouble" to witness to the coming of Christ to occupy the throne of David.

More observant readers of the Scripture will have noted that the tribe of Dan is not a part of these tribes as delineated by John. Dan was among the earliest of the tribes to go into idolatry and, for this reason, it is possible that the pseudo-Messiah may come out of this tribe (Genesis 49:17). Actually, there were thirteen tribes since Joseph's was divided between his two sons, Ephraim and Manasseh. In every list of the tribes, however, one of the groups is omitted. Usually it is Levi, the roving priest-tribe. Here it is Dan. Also, the name of Joseph is substituted for Ephraim.

Successful beyond our imagination will be these faithful witnesses. Following the sealing of the one hundred forty-four thousand, John envisions "a great multitude which no man could number, from every nation, from all tribes and peoples and tongues, standing before the throne and before the Lamb . . ." (Revelation 7:9 RSV). They are celebrating before the throne and singing praises to God. Then John is told that "these are they which came out of great tribulation, and have washed their robes and made them white in the blood of the Lamb" (7:14). Their rewards are enumerated and insured forever. Little doubt can surround the identity of this multitude. They are the Jews and Gentiles who have been led to Christ by the one hundred forty-four thousand during the awful days of the last week of prophecy.

Certainly, the Holy Spirit will be one with these witnesses. There could be no conversion to Christ without the initiation of that Spirit. We have earlier noted that the *Paraclete* (one called to go along beside, hence the Holy Spirit) has been removed at the time of the translation. While the Spirit, as the Church has known Him through Pentecost, will not be in the world during the last week, He will be here as the prophets of the Old Testament knew Him. A special relationship of the Spirit is reserved for the "Bride of Christ." It is this Spirit which inspired and motivated the prophets to prophesy the coming of the Messiah that will again be at work in the latter-day Jewish prophets.

An Apostate World Church Explodes

Towering over the people of the modern world is a monstrous conglomerate of ecclesiastical echelons who continue to insist that there must be one Church. It is to be worldwide with Catholics, Protestants, and Orthodox within its membership. Gradually, this highly-structured organization will begin to embrace non-Christian religions, religious groups as hostile to each other as Judaism and Islam. In this way the Kingdom of Heaven will dawn on earth and hostilities will be done away. The biblical foundation for the nature and mission of the Church will be subtly discarded in favor of a philosophical basis which extols the brotherhood of all people under the loving Fatherhood of a permissive God. No theology of any significance will be found at the center in the new and emerging World Church. The center will be pure humanism —a Narcissus complex in which man will love and adore himself. Naturally, such an institution of self-love under the disguise of selfless religion will be void of God and His Spirit. That fact seems to be beside the point for myriads of churchmen today.

Young Timothy was being groomed by the Apostle Paul to carry the torch after the martyrdom of his tutor in the faith. At the conclusion of the second letter written to him by Paul, there are warnings of such timely importance as to be worth quoting in this context. The apostle is discussing the latter days as he says,

> For the time is coming when people will not endure sound teaching, but having itching ears will accumulate for themselves

teachers to suit their own likings, and will turn away from listening
to the truth and wander into myths.

2 Timothy 4:3, 4 RSV

These words could be no more characteristic of our modern Church if
they had appeared in the morning newspaper. Ours is a period of
deepening apostasy in the institutional Church. It is this apostasy which
has initiated the drive to pool our weaknesses in an organization which
men believe will live longer because it is big!

Let no one think that the towering religious giant which has arisen
on the twentieth-century horizon is the first such tower in history. The
first was begun by men and women who lived shortly after the Great
Flood. It was constructed for the same reason that men are today
building an ecumenical organization of religion. Anything built to the
grandeur of man in the name of God is destined to collapse. The Tower
of Babel was never completed. The World Church of the present time
is so anti-Christian in its understanding of the purpose for which God
brought it into existence that it will suffer the same fate. Either it will
be shattered before it is completed (that is, before its dreams are realized) or it will think that it has achieved its humanistic goal only to be
exploded in the midst of its success.

A detailed description of the World Church existing during the first
half of the prophesied last week is given by Christ in His revelation to
John on Patmos. This false Church is called "the great harlot" and is
pictured "sitting on a scarlet beast which was full of blasphemous
names" (Revelation 17:1–3 RSV). At once we are made to understand
that this prostituted institution of religion is in alliance with the Beast
(Antichrist). In fact, in being depicted as *astride the Beast* we must
admit that the World Church is so powerful in the early days of the end
of the age as to enjoy a measure of control over the political system. Of
particular interest is the contrast between this unholy alliance and the
relationship between the true Church and its Messiah. The Church is
the *Bride* of the Christ while the apostate church married to the Antichrist is a prostitute.

Throughout the Scriptures the analogy of harlotry is employed to
illustrate a relationship with God which has been broken. Idolatry (wor-

ship of other gods) is nothing other than spiritual adultery. When this World Church is seen as a harlot, it is not difficult to conceive of what has happened. The harlot church has "committed fornication" with "the kings of the earth" (17:2), which means that the religious institution of that terrible time will have become the plaything of a secular, pagan world. Still claiming to be God's Church, the hierarchy and membership will be like an unfaithful wife pretending to be good only as a ruse. Religion wedded to worldliness is always harlotry.

Sometime around the middle of the week the Beast, on which the World Church has been riding, will throw off his rider. Joined by the decision of the subkings of the ten-nation confederacy of the Roman Empire, the Antichrist will suddenly destroy the entire religious organization. John's words are most descriptive:

> And the ten horns . . . and the beast will hate the harlot; they will make her desolate and naked, and devour her flesh and burn her up with fire, for God has put it into their hearts to carry out his purpose by being of one mind and giving over their royal power to the beast, until the words of God shall be fulfilled.
>
> Revelation 17:16, 17 RSV

What method will be used is unknown to us. From the graphic words used in this terse account, we might suspect that some form of nuclear energy will be employed to explode and burn the headquarters of the harlot. It would be done at a time when all the World Church leaders were present for a summit meeting called by the false prophet himself. Thus, in one stroke, the whole thing would be obliterated forever from the earth. And let us not overlook the stated fact that this is *God's judgment* on the adulterous World Church. It is only carried out by the Beast.

Identification of the Church

Revelation informs us that the Beast on which the harlot is seen sitting has "seven heads" (17:3) and that they represent "seven hills" (17:9). Though the mystery name of the harlot is "Babylon the great, mother of harlots and of earth's abominations" (17:5 RSV), we must not think of the ancient city of Babylon as being the location of the end-time church. Rather, Babylon was the symbol of the most loathsome and abominable forms of idolatry and shame. It was in the area of that city where the ancient Tower of Babel had been erected. The location is specifically said to be on "seven hills" and there is only one place in the world which has always been known by this description—the city of Rome. It stands to reason that the revived Roman Empire would have its capital in the same place as before. Rome will probably be both the capital of the political system and the headquarters of the World Church until the middle of the week when the Antichrist moves his capital to the desecrated Temple in Jerusalem and destroys the ecclesiastical headquarters in Rome!

Further insight is given when John writes, "And the woman that you saw is the great city which has dominion over the kings of the earth" (17:18 RSV). What city, in its religious preeminence, has ever fitted this description except Rome? But let us look once more at the picture.

> The woman was arrayed in purple and scarlet, and bedecked with gold and jewels and pearls, holding in her hand a golden cup full of abominations and the impurities of her fornication . . . And I saw the woman drunk with the blood of the saints and the blood of the martyrs of Jesus.
>
> Revelation 17:4, 6 RSV

Manifest to all is the fact that no organization of institutional religion at any time or any place has ever matched the wealth, luxury, and splendor of the church at Rome. How often has the religious persecution of Christians come from Rome!

A word of caution and clarification is needed before we proceed further. For many centuries there have been Christians who have been bitter toward their Catholic neighbors on the assumption that the Catholic church was the harlot of Revelation. Today, as prophecy is being fulfilled before our eyes, it is becoming clear that such an assumption was not entirely correct. Many Roman Catholics are discovering the personal Christ in these days and are seeking to bring renewal to their church on the pattern of the New Testament. This is also happening in practically every mainline denomination within Protestantism.

It is not the Roman Catholic Church *per se* which is to become the harlot in Revelation. Rather, it is a developing World Church embracing all religious viewpoints which will ultimately be absorbed into some ultra-corrupted form of the pre-Reformation Church. Catholic-Orthodox-Protestant dialogue is making this all too obvious. Little by little doctrinal and theological absolutes are being thrown aside as the Church moves nearer to reunion under one ecclesiastical ruler whose headquarters will be in the only reasonable place—Rome. It is the head of that apostate church—whether called *pope* or *doctor*—who will develop into the false prophet allied with Antichrist.

When the World Church is finally destroyed by the Beast it will be due to the fact that it has served its purpose in unifying the world around a pagan, secular, atheistic dictatorship. There will be no more need for it; therefore, the proud satanic ruler will annihilate it. No one will be too disturbed by its demolition. The Gentiles have little respect for the ecumenical movement today and will have even less interest in it after the translation of the true Church. Life will go on for a little while after the apostate World Church is gone just as though nothing had happened.

The Evil Winds Become a Storm

Through the first three and one-half years in the last phase of the present world order man will have observed some of history's most horrible catastrophes of nature multiplied in intensity a thousand times. The judgments revealed in the seals, trumpets, and vials stretch all across the seven years, but it is likely that the first six seals will be opened and fulfilled in the first half of the final prophetic week. Earlier we sought to identify the events under the first and second seals. The white horse and rider is the arrival of Antichrist followed by the red horse which John says means war. The third seal reveals a horse of a different color —black—and it represents famine. A natural result of war and famine is death, symbolized by the pale horse under the fourth seal. The fifth and sixth seals speak of terrible persecution against the Jews and a generalized upheaval in the forces of nature. The total picture is vividly painted in the sixth chapter of the Apocalypse.

If one is a careful student of the biblical record, he cannot have missed the amazing similarity between the seal's contents and the warning about the troubles of the end of the age as given by Jesus to the disciples in Matthew 24 (cf. Mark 13 also). In answer to their questions about the Second Coming of the Lord and the end of the existing world order, Jesus said essentially the same thing which John later sees on the isle of Patmos. He even follows the sequence of the six seals.

The first statement made by our Lord relating to the disciples query was, ". . . Take heed that no one leads you astray. For many will come in my name saying, 'I am the Christ,' and they will lead many astray" (vs. 4, 5 RSV). In verses 23 through 27 are found additional remarks about these "false Christs and false prophets." The disciples are emphatically told not to believe those who cry, "Here is the Christ!" or "There He is!" They are further informed that He will not be found "in the wilderness" or "in the inner rooms" but that His Coming will be like "lightning." This simply means that no one will have to look for the true Messiah in any one place. He will be visible to all in the heavens when He returns. Included in this warning were all the precursors of the last false Messiah who would purport to be Christ across the years. John says, ". . . the spirit of Antichrist . . . is in the world already" (1 John 4:3 RSV). The wickedness of them all will be combined in Satan's crowning effort to produce a perfect counterfeit of the Messiah.

Next, Jesus warns of the wars (vs. 6, 7) revealed under the second seal in Revelation. Then comes famines (v. 7) as prophesied in seal number three. Never in history have we seen so many famines with millions of starving people. Death (seal four) and persecution (seal five) are interwoven in a lengthy section (vs. 9–22) which includes the specific warning about the abomination of desolation. The catastrophes mentioned in connection with the sixth seal are recorded in apocalyptic fashion in verse 29. From this point in Matthew's twenty-fourth chapter our Lord describes His return to earth and gives careful clarification as to what should be expected as signs preceding the coming in judgment. The whole chapter is at the center of the prophecies relating to the end as found in both the Old and New Testaments.

8
The Dawn of the Kingdom of Man

A Merger of Civil and Religious Power

By the start of the second phase of the last prophetic week on earth, the Antichrist will have everything going his way. The last vestige of ecclesiastical institutionalism will be gone and "the final solution to the Jewish problem" shall appear to have been achieved. In abject fear of the demonic dictator's invincible strength and in a hypnotic state of hero worship, the world's peoples are by this juncture in time fully committed to the Beast. The loyal patriotism felt by the citizens of the universal kingdom of Antichrist easily comes to include an attitude of divine worship. Once again the Caesar of the revived Roman Empire sees everyone bowing and, with great emotion reminiscent of the early days of Christianity, crying, "Caesar is Lord!" Patriotism and religion —no better combination has ever been found to cement together a world which is always falling apart. And the zenith of perfection has arrived when both the patriotism and worship are centered in one person.

Everybody knows much earlier that the head of the World Church is a powerful man. It had been noised abroad that he possessed supernatural powers like the prophets of old. The Antichrist was personally aware of this and, through the first three and one-half years, had cultivated a friendship which grew into a kind of king-advisor relationship. Together they had plotted the betrayal of the Jewish nation and the destruction of the World Church. The understanding was that the two of them could work together much better as a team if the cumbersome institutions could be discarded. It was in exchange for the second seat in the kingdom that the head of the World Church agreed to set up the meeting of religious leaders in Rome when the explosion had occurred.

John sees this religious personage rise "out of the earth" as the powerful representative of the Antichrist (Revelation 13:11–18). Its appearance is that of "another beast" with "two horns like a lamb" and a voice "like a dragon." At once the duplicity of its nature is observed. His appearance is a striking imitation of "the Lamb of God who takes away the sin of the world" (John 1:29). All through Revelation Christ is portrayed as a Lamb (5:6; 6:1; 7:9; 12:11; 13:8; 14:1; 15:3; 17:14; 22:1; etc.) and Satan takes advantage of the Messiah's characteristics to dupe the masses. The strategic aspect to note, however, is that, though he tries to look like the Lamb of God, he is actually a beast. No two animal dispositions could be more irreconcilable. And the clincher as to the real nature of the beast is when we hear him speak "like a dragon." As Christ is symbolized in Revelation as a Lamb, so Satan is portrayed as a dragon (12:3, 4, 7, 9, 16; 13:2; 16:13; 20:2). Thus we have a description of a false prophet, which the second beast is called later (16:13), as one who tries to look and act like the Lord but actually articulates the words and will of Satan. That combination has deceived men and women since the beginning of time!

The work of the false prophet is said to be that of enhancing the reign of the Beast by building up his image in the people's minds and drawing attention to his greatness. Pointedly, the second beast "exercises all the authority of the first beast in its presence and makes the earth and its inhabitants worship the first beast . . ." (13:12). In order to do this, the Pandora's box of demonic powers is opened by Satan and its contents are given to the false prophet. For he will work "great signs, even making fire come down from heaven to earth in the sight of men" (v. 13). Charisma will abound in its most evil form, and the scientific, magic, and demonic wonders which he performs will be all but impossible to resist. If we recall that the false prophet is the third person of the unholy trinity and the antithesis of the Holy Spirit, we will see the reason for the use of heavenly fire. It was the Spirit of God who, on the day of Pentecost, descended with tongues of fire on the disciples (Acts 2:3). And it will be in an attempt to duplicate that powerful moment that the lesser beast manipulates the powers committed to him.

Technologized Idolatry

Legerdemain is the art of deceiving by sleight of hand. Everyone enjoys an evening with a good magician. We are awed and mystified by his uncanny ability to fool us. Surely there will be some of this kind of thing involved in the work of the greatest legerdemainist ever to appear on the stage of human history. Yet, there is more to it than just magic —far more. We have witnessed in this century how science and technology can be either a blessing or a curse on mankind. It all depends on who uses it and how. When the marvels of our technological and scientific world get into the hands of a wild, demon-possessed, power-crazed man, the entire earth is in for trouble. In retrospect, one sees how perilously close the world came to such a fate in the nearly perfected V-2 rocket of Nazi Germany!

When the false prophet appears on the scene he will have total control of the discoveries of scientific and technological laboratories. Combining this power with a mystic, cultic aura will be a trick the likes of which none can dream .The Scriptures say that the people will be led to "make an image for the beast" (Revelation 13:14). Nothing suprising about that. How often in the past have men built images to worship? Look at the Israelites at the foot of Sinai (Exodus 32), the Egyptians' imagery in stone still observed in the ancient ruins, the huge statue erected by Nebuchadnezzar on the plain of Dura (Daniel 3), the numerous idols of the Greeks and Romans. Some of these latter gods and goddesses in stone have been found to contain conduits running underground to the priests quarters from which the voice of the image came to dupe the worshipers. Strikingly enough, the people in the last days will be deceived by another such talking image.

On the day when the Beast's image is dedicated in the Temple on Mount Zion (the abomination of desolation mentioned by Daniel and Jesus), the false prophet will pull off his most spectacular hoax. In the solemn ceremony attended by hundreds of thousands of excited people, suddenly the image will take on the appearance of being alive. Nowhere does the Scripture say that the image *does* come to life. This will not be the case. What will happen is that the statue will move and the sound of a voice will be heard coming from it. Probably, the figure will be artificially animated like the waxed presidents at Florida's Disney World. The lifelike visage and movements of the figures coordinated with the recorded voice will make the sight almost eerie. With access to the wonders of science and technology, which will be even more advanced by the time of the Beast, there will be no end to the numbers of ways by which the image will seem alive. And under the power of suggestion being handled by the greatest magician, wisest wizard, most capable scientist, and wickedest demon, it is normal to expect the worshiping people to believe anything.

After rejection of the truth for a long enough time, men finally get to the point where they cannot distinguish between truth and error. Jesus cautioned the Pharisees about this (Matthew 12:22–32) when they could not decide whether the Lord was doing His work by the power of God or the power of the devil. And Paul, discoursing on the days of "the lawless one" when there will be "pretended signs and wonders," flatly states, "Therefore, God sends upon them a strong delusion, to make them believe what is false" (2 Thessalonians 2:8–12 RSV). Such is the punishment deserved by men and women who refuse the truth of God and reject the light of His Son. It is no wonder that these people will believe the lies of the false prophet when they have no inner standard of truth by which to check themselves. His wonders will look so genuine, his appearance so religious. Early in His ministry, the Master warned about men like the beast "who come to you in sheep's clothing but inwardly are ravening wolves" (Matthew 7:15). That statement brings a flashback of the description of the false prophet in Revelation where he is seen with "two horns like a lamb."

A Special Brand of People

Working in close cooperation with the Antichrist who dwells in sheltered security within the Temple precincts in Jerusalem, the false prophet enforces the order of the Beast that all people shall bow before the animated image. Anyone refusing to comply will be killed at once. No leniency, no trial, no mercy. The word of the dictator on Mount Zion is law—inflexible and irrevocable! Only the one hundred forty-four thousand Jewish witnesses previously sealed by God (Revelation 7:1–8; 14:1–5) will be spared.

The alternative to death will be a brand upon one's flesh similar to that inflicted on cattle grazing on unfenced lands. A brand indicates ownership and the right of the owner to dispose of his property as he wills. Once the mark of ownership has been burnt into the flesh it cannot be removed. Henceforth, the die is cast and the marked slave has no more right to his own decisions. John envisions the brand being infused on either the forehead or the right hand. Without the dictator's mark one will be unable to engage in any kind of business, not even the purchase of food or clothing. Secret police will cover the earth like flies on a decaying carcass. It shall be their duty to seek out and put to death those who are disloyal.

A most illuminating explanation is given in the Apocalypse as to the meaning of the brand. The mark is a number and is equivalent to the name of the Antichrist. In one short verse we are told to use our heads ("This calls for wisdom") and "reckon the number of the beast, for it is a human number, its number is six hundred and sixty-six" (13:18 RSV). Varied and ingenious have been the suggested solutions to the proper understanding of this verse. It is a fact that numerical values were given by the Jews to each letter in the Hebrew alphabet. By adding the letters in one's name his number could be determined. When it is remembered that the Beast in Revelation is yet future it is recognized that knowing his name is of little significance. By the time he is announced as world ruler the populace will know who he is and what his name may be. To know that beforehand would change nothing since history is destined to run amuck under his reign.

To know the name is unimportant, but to know the kind of person he will be is of prime significance to the study of prophecy. Already we have seen that he is *anti*everything that has anything to do with God. *Anti* is a prefix meaning *against* and the Beast is decidedly against Christ, the nation of Israel (though at first he deceives the Jews with a treaty), and all forms of religion. He is the antithesis of Christ, always striving to emulate Him but only under the power of a reversing demonic spirit. Christ's ministry lasted about three and one-half years and the reign of Antichrist will cover the same period of time. Christ was God, but He made Himself man. Antichrist is man, but he makes himself God. And it is at this point where the number of his name becomes extremely enlightening.

The most sacred number among the Jews was the number *seven*. This was the symbol of perfection or completion. Therefore, the Bible speaks of "seven men" to be appointed deacons in the Ancient Church (Acts 6:3), forgiving "seven times" (Matthew 18:21), "seven churches" and "seven spirits" (Revelation 1:4), and "seven angels" (15:1, 6). In each instance the perfect number suggests completion. But, especially did *seven* refer to God. What could be more perfect or complete than He? In this sense, it became a divine number for Him who created the earth in six days and rested on the seventh. For the early apostles there was no doubt about the deity of Christ. Obviously, then, the number seven belonged to Him as well as to the Father.

Man's number was *six*. It was on the sixth day of creation that he was brought into existence. Being God's masterpiece and the highest order of earth's creatures, he deserved a place next to God. Numerically, that would have to be six if God is seven. Our first insight into the Beast's identity, then, is in discovering that the number of man is six. That is as high as he can go. But why three sixes (666)? In the Church of the New Testament era the concept of the Trinity arose. It developed out of two facts. The Old Testament uses the plural form of the word for God by which the Hebrews insisted that all gods were summed up in the one true *Jehovah Elohim*. There was no queston about God the Father in the minds of the apostles. Then they discovered that Jesus shared that Godhead and, shortly after His Ascension, that the Holy Spirit did as well. Thus the God who is "three-in-one" became the Christian way of explaining God's full-orbed Being. Three is, therefore, the number of the Trinity. In light of this, God's number may be said to be 777.

We have seen in a preceding section of our study that Satan tries to counterfeit the Godhead during the last prophetic week with the Dragon, the Beast, and the false prophet. So we have a trinity here, too. From this it is easy enough to see what happened. Antichrist will try to be God. With every ounce of energy that he has and every deceptive strategy which he can muster, he will insist that he is divine. Even the devil-head of "three-in-one" is employed. But, alas, it does not work. He is still only a man whose number is six. And combining all the persons of his reign (Satan, Antichrist, and the false prophet) results in 666—

an extension of his power but not an amplification of his nature into divinity. Only God is 777. Try as he will, the Beast will never usurp God's throne. Thus 666 is the number of a man—an exalted and powerful man—but still a man.

God's Final Appeal

Two special witnesses, in addition to the one hundred forty-four thousand, are to sound the Word of God for three and one-half years (Revelation 11:3–13). Whether this is to be in the first or the last half of the final prophetic week on earth is uncertain. It is the opinion of this writer that, since divine protection is needed, the witnesses are active in the last rather than the first part of the seven-year period. It is in the last half that the tribulation becomes most severe. They are dressed in sackcloth which implies that they are pronouncing doom upon the world and calling for repentance. They are further said to be "the two olive trees and the two lampstands" (11:4), an apparent reference to the fourth chapter of the Book of Zechariah. There Joshua and Zerubbabel were the witnesses nourished with divine power symbolized by the olive oil. Here, in this time of trouble, God raises up two men again to be energized by the Spirit of the Lord to proclaim the coming Kingdom and its judgment on the wicked.

From the signs which they are enabled to perform we are inevitably led to think of Moses and Elijah who did similar things in the past. "They have power over the waters to turn them into blood, and to smite the earth with every plague . . ." (11:6 RSV.) These words are strikingly familiar from the work of Moses as recorded in Exodus 7:17–19. ". . .fire pours from their mouth and consumes their foes . . ." (11:5 RSV) and "They have power to shut the sky, that no rain may fall during the days of their prophesying . . ." (11:6 RSV). That sounds precisely like the prophetic ministry of Elijah (2 Kings 1:11, 12) and particularly the occasion of his restraining the rain for exactly three and one-half years (1 Kings. 17:1; 18:1; cf. James 5:17, 18).

As a prelude to His coming Davidic Kingdom, Jesus was transfigured in the presence of three of His disciples. In the midst of the breathtaking experience appeared Moses and Elijah (Matthew 17:3). Since they are related to the coming *parousia* in the Gospel of Matthew, there is good reason to associate them with these end-time prophets. Furthermore, Malachi said that God would send "Elijah the prophet before the coming of the great and dreadful day of the Lord" (Malachi 4:5). This prophecy must have begun to come to pass in John the Baptist who announced the first coming of the King since Jesus calls him Elijah (Matthew 17:12; Mark 9:13). However, it is reasonable to assume that the rejection of both John and Christ may demand the return of both in the end-time. One other point should be noted: Moses and Elijah stand for the best of the law and the prophets. What could be more appropriate than that the spokesmen of the law and the prophets should once again prophesy before the final realization of the Kingdom of David?

More important than their identity is their ministry and fate. Unquestionably, these two witnesses are sent as God's final appeal for men to repent. Divine patience is so inexhaustible that the Lord tries again and again. He even refuses to allow the witnesses to be killed until the three and one-half years come to an end. Beyond that point there is no more opportunity for repentance so the prophetic witnesses are slain in the city of Jerusalem. Great joy attends their deaths and in order to give all people a chance to see the victory of the Beast, they remain unburied for over three days. Suddenly, after three days, they are raised from the dead and ascend into heaven. Terror grips the hearts of the people as they are poignantly reminded that God will have the last word. At that moment, the land is shaken by an earthquake and seven thousand people are killed. Such earthquakes will not be uncommon in the great tribulation.

The Fall of the Secular City

Continually, the world is hearing more and more about the glory of the bulging metropolis. Cities are overcrowded, dirty, polluted, and filled with wickedness and corruption. Presumably, the Creator never intended that men should live in the incredibly difficult conditions of the modern city. The first attempt to build a city was by the vagabond Cain (Genesis 4:17). Nothing is known of his success and it is possible that

God brought his efforts to naught as he was cursed because of his sin to be a wanderer and fugitive from justice. The second known attempt to create city life was connected with the erection of the Tower of Babel (Genesis 11) which was cut short by a visit from Jehovah! Later, on that spot, a city was constructed which has come to be synonymous with all that is bad about city life. It is still remembered as Babylon the Great. And it is this name which the angel gives to the political and commercial metropolis of the last days on earth.

Increasingly, the model for our modern cities with their sardine-pressed populations is that of ancient Babylon. Evil permeates every facet of the big city. Crime is concentrated there and immorality becomes a way of life. In our cities is where ghetto existence becomes intolerable. Yet, multitudes continue to migrate to the urban areas in spite of the fact that we know how unwholesome they are. In the event of nuclear attack the worst place would be in the city for the warheads would be directed to the most heavily-populated segments of society. Someday the cities will be demolished. And in their place God will construct the New Jerusalem.

The Babylon in chapter eighteen of the Book of Revelation is the political and commercial center of the world in the days of the great tribulation. It, like the ecclesiastical structure by the same name, will most probably be located in Rome. All commerce will pass through its offices and be either approved or rejected by computerized processing which detects the least trace of disloyalty. Economic controls will branch out from Rome like the arms of an octopus to choke and restrict all political and commercial enterprises. Totally godless and devoid of conscience, every man will be for himself in a struggle to survive.

When the devastation of the city of man comes near the end of the last three and one-half years, it will be complete. The pride of science and technology will be utterly deflated forever in the holocaust which leaves the metropolis in irreparable ruins. "The kings of the earth, who committed fornication and were wanton with her, will weep and wail over her when they see the smoke of her burning" (Revelation 18:9 RSV). The merchants and seafarers from afar join their laments to that of the kings in their shock at the suddenness with which the heart of their existence has been crushed. "In one hour has thy judgment come

. . . in one hour all this wealth has been laid waste" (18:10, 17 RSV).

Silence, nothing but silence, can depict the city in the wake of its cataclysmic disaster from the hand of God. The evil city is haunted by the deathly silence which John sees settle over the smoldering wasteland.

> and the sound of harpers and minstrels,
> of flute players and trumpeters,
> shall be heard in thee no more;
> and a craftsman of any craft
> shall be found in thee no more;
> and the sound of the millstone
> shall be heard in thee no more;
> and the light of a lamp
> shall shine in thee no more;
> and the voice of bridegroom and bride
> shall be heard in thee no more . . . .
>
> Revelation 18–23 RSV

Over the silence of earth's metropolitan doomsday will be heard the mighty voice of the heavenly throng, crying, "Hallelujah! Salvation and glory and power belong to our God . . . Hallelujah! The smoke from her goes up forever and ever . . . Hallelujah! For the Lord God the Almighty reigns" (19:1, 3, 6 RSV). Once again the population of the earth will be greatly decreased as multiplied millions perish in the corrupted city of Babylon, the revived political and commercial center of the ancient empire of the Caesars. Of couse, nothing can ever so quickly curtail ecological problems as the eradication of the pollution-producing cities!

The Sound of Judgment

The "silence in heaven for about half an hour" (8:1 RSV), which comes between the events of the sixth seal and the blowing of the seven trumpets contained in the seventh seal, probably indicates a break in the seven years of trouble. Not only is this a brief respite arranged by a patient God, but it suggests the momentous beginning of the last half of the "time of Jacob's trouble." Thus we get a glimpse into judgments of far more serious consequences as the trumpets blow and the bowls of wrath are emptied (8:7–16:21). Since the entire universe is scheduled to lose its equilibrium under the fierce sway of the satanic hordes, the tragedies depicted in these chapters are not hard to believe. As the first trumpet blows the earth is bombarded with a mixture of hail, fire, and blood which burns a third of the earth. Blazing meteors are featured in the next two plagues which destroy a third of the ships at sea and poison and bloody the oceans until one-third of the fish are killed. The fourth trumpet blast partially obscures the light of the sun, moon, and stars fulfilling the prediction of Jesus.

> "and there will be signs in the sun and moon and stars, and upon the earth distress of nations in perplexity at the roaring of the sea and the waves, men fainting with fear and with foreboding of what is coming on the world; for the powers of the heavens will be shaken.
>
> Luke 21:25, 26 RSV

The first four trumpets will be strangely reminiscent of the plagues inflicted on Egypt because of the mistreatment of the Hebrew slaves. Supposedly, these tragedies are to be leveled at the earth again for the same reason. In the remaining trinity of trumpets (referred to as *woes* because the judgments are pronounced against man rather than the earth and seas) human life will be viciously attacked by venomous scorpions and a demonic-empowered army of two hundred million troops who will slay a third of all humanity. If this should transpire near the end of the twentieth century it is credible, on the basis of projected population estimates, that nearly two and one-half billion people would die. The population explosion seems to become less and less of a problem.

The seventh trumpet (third woe) specifically announces an earthquake which seriously shatters Jerusalem, killing seven thousand Jews, and driving masses of frightened citizens into the mountains. Assuredly, there is a relationship here to the words of Jesus, ". . . let those who are in Judea flee to the mountains" (Matthew 24:16) and "The days are coming when they will say . . . to the mountains, Fall on us; and to the hills, Cover us" (Luke 23:29, 30). It is possible that the mountains referred to may be the old capital of Edom across the Jordan River, a rock citadel known as Petra which was formerly a notable fortress. Nestled in the natural rock formations the fleeing Jews would have the best chance of hiding.

Involved in the third woe announced by the seventh trumpet are seven bowls of wrath to be poured out on the world. Followers of Antichrist will contract a malignant disease which will produce loathsome pustules on their flesh. All ocean life dies and even the rivers and springs of fresh water become red with blood. With no water to drink the sun's heat will blister mankind. Darkness will follow, perhaps because of an eclipse. In preparation for an invasion of Israel from the east, the Euphrates River will dry up and the Battle of Armageddon will be only days away. The hail which crumbles mighty buildings is probably associated with the destruction of political and commercial city life and the divine victory in the Valley of Megiddo. The population problem will soon be over.

9
The Last Great Global War

A War to End Wars?

Unanimous agreement prevailed among men of state from every civilized nation on earth that there must never be another world war. That was in 1945 when the last so-called global conflict was suddenly ended with explosions of the atomic bomb over two Japanese cities. The bombing was so inhumane in its widespread destruction that even scientists were shocked by what they saw. Buildings disintegrated and human bodies disappeared like released gas in the heart of the explosion. Solid steel melted as if it were wax held over a flame. Where once had been a modern city nothing remained except the blackened earth and scattered traces of rising steam. An entire city had become a cemetery— a ghost town of the past. Great numbers of people in outlying areas were killed or permanently affected by the swirls of radioactive dust. For many years to come the soil itself would be damaged in its ability to function. Even children born to men and women who had gone through the tragedy at its outer fringes would be crippled or mentally maimed due to their parents' radioactive impairment.

World War II was to be the war to end all wars. Humanity could never afford another. For a quarter of a century every major nation and numerous small countries have been negotiating through international channels to avoid cosmic nuclear war. Yet, entering the atomic weaponry race are new nations, some of them formerly thought quite primitive. No longer underdeveloped, they now have the ability to launch a vicious nuclear attack. Nuclear testings continue and arsenals keep on growing. All over the globe we have seen small-scale wars break out, some of them dragging into many years and involving the loss of many lives and an expenditure of exorbitant amounts of money. Innocent women, children, and aged have suffered untold anguish and suffering in these wars. Starvation is not an abnormal state for the populace of any such nation on whose soil war is pursued.

Every precaution has been taken to insure that these small-scale wars do not escalate to the frenzied pitch which could precipitate the use of nuclear energy by some capable and desperate despotic ruler. This could be one of the countries engaged in the battle, an uninvolved country which does no more than supply weapons, or a nation completely detached but who decides to take advantage of an opportune moment to become ruler of the world. Everyone who begins to comprehend the horrors of nuclear war is convinced that a third global war is out of the question. It would be the end of everything.

Ominous Things Ahead

According to the Scriptures (which have never yet been proved wrong), man will be incapable of keeping the peace which he so fervently seeks. The reason is plain to see. Peace among nations is an outward sign of an inward condition. No amount of peace planning and talking can substitute for the civil war which goes on inside the hearts of men. Man, in his unregenerate state, is seething with tension and friction stimulated by unfulfilled desires. This is what causes conflicts between neighbors and finally between nations. James puts it well: "What causes wars, and what causes fightings among you? Is it not your passions that are at war in your members? You desire and do not have; so you kill. And you covet and cannot obtain; so you fight and wage war . . ." (James 4:1, 2 RSV). To work for international peace when personal peace is lacking is like holding back the steam in a pressure cooker with an airtight lid. Eventually, the top will blow!

The theology which has usurped the throne for many years in the nineteenth and twentieth centuries insists that the world is getting better and better. All one needs is two eyes to know that this old humanism is built on a false foundation. No one in his right mind could think that the situation in the world is improving. The reason this humanistic optimism is collapsing like a house of cards is because it failed to seriously consider the Word of God. When a concept of life is constructed on man's philosophy rather than on revealed truth it is doomed for failure. For awhile such sugarcoated promises encourage mankind to develop its vast potential through an intensive exposure to science and education. Usually a sizeable crowd joins the idolatrous worshipers of man's ego-image. It becomes the popular way. Then the sweet bubble bursts in the prickly world of human sin and everybody wonders where we went wrong.

Had we been more intent across the years on knowing what the prophetic Word of God has to say, we would have spared ourselves much heartbreak and disillusionment. Very few people today have any sensible understanding of biblical prophecy. This is because our present generation has grown up on a religious and secular diet which lacks one of the vitamins essential to wholeness. We are obese with man's wisdom but frail and anemic where it really counts. If we had only taken Jesus seriously we would never have expected the world to get better. Referring to the last events on earth prior to His return in judgment, He clearly explains:

> And you will hear of wars and rumors of wars; see that you are not alarmed; for this must take place, but the end is not yet. For nation will rise against nation, and kingdom against kingdom . . . this is but the beginning of the sufferings.
>
> Matthew 24:6–8; Mark 13:7, 8 RSV

Throughout the writings of the Hebrew prophets, one is struck again and again by the repetitious predictions of an earth-shattering war at the end of time which will involve all the peoples of the earth. Of such specific character are these words that one can only think of all past wars as having been child's play. Zechariah writes of that war:

> On that day I will make Jerusalem a heavy stone for all the peoples; all who lift it shall grievously hurt themselves. And all the nations of the earth will come together against it.
>
> Zechariah 12:3 RSV

> In the whole land, says the Lord,
>   two thirds shall be cut off and perish,
>   and one third shall be left alive.
> And I will put this third into the fire,
>   and refine them as one refines silver,
>   and test them as gold is tested. . . .
>
> vs. 13:8, 9 RSV

The devastation and death will be so unbelievable in this last conflict in which all nations are engaged that over 65 percent of the world's population will be killed. It must be remembered that the teeming peoples of the world will already have been greatly decimated. But it will be this last battle that will solve the problem of overpopulation once and for all time.

The Spark Which Ignites the Fire

As the kingdom of man nears the final stages of its existence it will begin to fall apart. Puppet kings in the north, south, and east will grow restless with the ominous things happening everywhere. Even the subject rulers of the revived Roman Empire (there may be only seven left by this time—Daniel 7:8) shall have become so restive in their suspicion that the Antichrist, snug in his Temple in Jerusalem, has betrayed the world that they will rise up in revolt. Under a kind of obsession for self-destruction the nations will pour fuel on their distrust of each other. Disunity will prevail in the ranks. Men everywhere will be grumbling because the promises of brotherhood and plenty offered to them early in the last prophetic week have been gradually broken. No one shall know for certain who should be blamed for the shambles that characterize the world. Thus every nation will suspect its neighbor and the spark which creates all wars will suddenly ignite a holocaust so gigantic that the scene will be an amplified repeat of the destruction of Sodom and Gomorrah (Genesis 19:24–28).

Coupled with this growing disillusionment with the kingdom of man as brought into being by the sinfulness of human solidarity will be an unquenchable hatred for the land of Palestine and its peoples. Some will start the rumor that the Jews, favored earlier by the dictator, are responsible for the desolation that is coming upon the nations. We have heard that kind of reasoning before. And there is a sense in which it is true since the restored State of Israel plays a leading role in this ultimate battle. Recognizing the explosive nature of the situation, and knowing that too many people are involved for him ever to exterminate them all, the Antichrist will take advantage of the rumor for selfish ends. To do so will turn the attention of the world to the despised Jews and eliminate the suspicion which some feel toward the Beast himself. Making it all appear to be his own idea, the Antichrist will declare war on the Israelites and seek again to unify his empire in a common cause.

The Jews have always stood for God and His intrusion in the world in the minds of men and women who despise the way of righteousness. In every attempt to destroy the Hebrew people there has been an underlying, subtle attack upon God. In this light the final cosmic war must be seen as the long-planned confrontation between the kingdom of man—championed by Satan—and the Kingdom of God—championed by the Lord Christ. Long ago the psalmist foresaw this conflict coming when he penned in graphic words,

> Why do the nations conspire,
> and the peoples plot in vain?
> The kings of the earth set themselves,
> and the rulers take counsel together,
> against the Lord and his anointed, saying
> "Let us burst their bonds asunder,
> and cast their cords from us."
>
> Psalms 2:1–3 RSV

The spark is a twofold thing growing out of disenchantment with the decaying utopia of man's ingenuity and deception and the release of centuries of anti-Semitism in the hearts of the world's last generation of citizens. With a burning hatred of God there is always a smoldering hatred of men. Where this is the situation in its most intensified form since the beginning of the human race, global war is unavoidable.

Behind the Scene

Let none of us forget that our God is sovereign. Nothing takes Him by surprise nor does any man or nation do anything without divine permission. This is not to say that the Eternal Spirit is responsible for the mess into which we get ourselves and our world, but it is to affirm dogmatically that nothing can ever happen unless He allows it. This is His universe and He is in charge. Satan and his emissaries are permitted to go only so far with their plans (cf. Job 1:6–12). Man, under the influence of this Evil Spirit, will also be checked when God decides to terminate his wickedness.

One of the amazing revelations of Scripture is the way in which God can turn the evil of man into the fulfillment of the divine plan. Man, in his rebellion, can only destroy himself—never God! When he disobeys the commands of the Lord the only thing which is broken is the man—never the eternal laws of the universe. When Pharaoh "hardened his heart" (Exodus 8:15) against the will of Jehovah for His people, the Lord used the king's rebellion to bring glory to the divine plan of the ages. Moses states that "the Lord hardened Pharaoh's heart . . ." (10:20) which can only imply that God used the Egyptian ruler's proud rejection to carry out the sovereign design of the Creator. God will have His way and He has invited man to share in the unfolding plan. When man rejects that way of truth he changes nothing about the ultimate design. He only *chooses* to be a cog in the machinery of the universe rather than a son in the House of the Lord.

Precisely the same thing happened at Calvary where Satan and his followers were sure that they had defeated the plan of God. All they did in crucifying the Lord of glory was to bring about the redemption of the lost world. The cross was not Satan's idea, nor was it man's. It was God's!

Likewise, the ultimate conflict among the nations of the world, as they gather in miserable disarray to flatten the people of Israel and demolish the last trace of God from the earth, is all a part of the plan of God. One cannot read the Scriptures without seeing this impossible-to-overlook truth. None of this which will happen is what He wants. God's original plan was to create a world of righteousness and peace for man and all the creatures of the earth. But man's sin has brought into existence an evil order which must be ended. God has been more than longsuffering with mankind, both Jew and Gentile. He has even told us what the signs of the end will be so that none need be caught unprepared. Therefore, for those who reject the Saviour and spurn God's love, there is nothing left but disaster. And that disaster is as much God's doing as the cross was His idea.

Joel hears distinctly this great truth that God is involved in the final global war when he shares the revelation that he has received. His words are concise and crystal clear:

> Proclaim this among the nations:
> Prepare war,
> > stir up the mighty men.
> Let all the men of war draw near,
> > let them come up.
> Beat your plowshares into swords,
> > and your pruning hooks into spears;
> > let the weak say, "I am a warrior."
>
> Hasten and come,
> > all you nations round about,
> > gather yourselves there.
> Bring down thy warriors, O LORD.
> Let the nations bestir themselves,
> > and come up to the valley of Jehoshaphat;
> for there I will sit to judge
> > all the nations round about.
>
> Joel 3:9–12 RSV

Zechariah hears the same thing in his oracle concerning Jerusalem and the coming universal reign of Christ on David's throne. God Himself is speaking:

> I will gather all the nations against Jerusalem to battle, and the city shall be taken and the houses plundered and the women ravished; half of the city shall go into exile, but the rest of the people

shall not be cut off from the city. Then the Lord will go forth and
fight against those nations as when he fights on a day of battle.

Zechariah 14:2, 3 RSV

Behind the scene of destruction stands God, like the Ancient of Days,
commanding the whole battle and calling every shot. It is His world, His
battle, and His victory! Dare any mortal mind question the wisdom of
the rightness of the acts of the Lord?

A Battleground Made Ready

Just as surely as the Bible accurately predicted the place of Jesus' birth
(Micah 5:2) so the prophetic Scriptures tell us precisely where this great
war will be fought. Even now the Middle East is being prepared for the
coming conflict. Where else could the final showdown between God and
Satan possibly occur than on the holy soil of Palestine? Human rebellion
will be crushed near the place where it first appeared. The traditional
location of the Garden of Eden is no more than five hundred miles due
east of Jerusalem. And what is much more important, it was in this area
that God began to create a chosen nation with the call of Abraham from
the general area of Eden. The land of Canaan (Palestine or Israel)
became the seedbed for the growing of the new covenant people. There
the Kingdom began and there it will be ultimately established. The great
war will be Satan's best strategy which has been in the process of being
designed for four thousand years. All the stops will be pulled out and
the winner will take all!

From a practical standpoint alone the last war will have to take place
in Palestine. Scientists tell us that the nations of the world are rapidly
depleting their resources. Soon they will be gone. Yet, the little land of
Palestine, almost untouched for the past four millennia in so far as its
underground minerals are concerned, holds enough needed reserves in
petroleum and chemical deposits to supply the entire world for at least
another thousand years. In addition, the Jews are returning to this land
with their massive wealth. Can there be any doubt that God has seen
to it that the Jews are not only preserved but also made wealthy for the
time of this conflict? (Cf. Isaiah 60:5–9; Ezekiel 38:11–13). Israel will

be completely independent, the richest nation on earth. Is it any wonder that the world's peoples (solely from a practical viewpoint) will decide to attack this smug little land?

Joel refers to the valley of Jehoshaphat (Joel 3:12) as the site of the war of the nations. No actual valley in pre-Christian days bore this name, but it is generally agreed by biblical scholars that the reference is a figurative use of a word denoting the place of divine judgment on the nations. The precise naming of the place of battle is done by John in the Apocalypse.

> And I saw . . . three foul spirits . . . demonic spirits, performing signs, who go abroad to the kings of the whole world, to assemble them for battle on the great day of God the Almighty. . . . And they assembled them at a place which is called in Hebrew Armageddon.
>
> Revelation 16:13–16 RSV

Armageddon is a combination of two Hebrew words: *har* (hill) and *Megiddo*, the name of a mount or city on the southern elevated edge of the plain of Esdraelon, known to history as the most famous battlefield in the land of Canaan. There Barak defeated the Canaanites (Judges 4:15) and Gideon routed the Midianites (Judges 7). There also Saul met his death (1 Samuel 31:4–8) and Josiah came to the tragic end of his life (2 Kings 23:29, 30; 2 Chronicles 35:22–24). This noted battlefield at the foot of the mountain is twenty-two miles long and about fifteen miles wide. It should be noted that, while the heart of the conflict will be in this plain designed as an ideal field of battle, the deployment of troops will cover a wide area of as much as two hundred miles (cf. Revelation 14:20).

The expression, "The Battle of Armageddon," strikes terror in the hearts of people everywhere. Little knowledge of the Bible is needed for the words to conjure images of bloodshed and massacre. People who have learned nothing of its biblical and prophetic importance are innately aware that Armageddon speaks of something more horrible than they have ever known. Scientists and military men often refer to the approach of Armageddon to describe their anticipation of fearful events to come. Even poets and novelists employ the word to depict ultimate and irreversible conflict.

The Tide Turns Against the Kingdom of Man

Madness will possess the troops in the plain of Megiddo. John speaks of "a great earthquake such as had never been since men were on the earth . . ." (Revelation 16:18 RSV) which disrupts the strategy of battle by throwing men into a panic. If we recall the second woe under the sixth trumpet (9:13–16) we will note that an army of two hundred million men will invade Israel from beyond the dried-up Euphrates River. It is interesting to note that China claims exactly that number of troops ready for combat today! When the armies from the western confederacy, the north, and the south are added to this vast horde, one can imagine what pandemonium will exist. Men and implements of war will be jammed against one another only to be thrown into futher disarray with an earthquake. The result can be anticipated even now. In fact, prophets saw it long ago. Zechariah says it like this: "And on that day a great panic from the Lord shall fall on them, so that each will lay hold on the hand of his fellow, and the hand of the one will be raised against the hand of the other; even Judah will fight against Jerusalem . . ." (Zechariah 14:13, 14 RSV). Haggai writes of the same confusion in battle, ". . . the horses and their riders shall go down, everyone by the sword of his fellow . . ." (Haggai 2:22 RSV).

In the general upheaval of nature accompanying the earthquake will be indescribable horrors from the heavens. Ezekiel, in his vision of the judgment of God upon Gog, says, "With pestilence and bloodshed I will enter in judgment with him; and I will rain upon him and his hordes and the many peoples that are with him, torrential rains and hailstones, fire and brimstone" (Ezekiel 38:22 RSV). If this is to be done to Russia and her allies in the earlier invasion during the last seven years, how much more severe may we expect the divine wrath to be when poured out upon all rebel nations combined!

The fire and brimstone which *rained* upon Sodom and Gomorrah (Genesis 19:24) was molten pitch from the bitumen pits at the rim of the Dead Sea set ablaze by the explosions of the sulphur mines in the area. Falling upon men, the burning mass completely charred all flesh. With the earthquake in the end-times there naturally will be volcanic eruptions of mighty force which can create the same conditions for the multitudes in the plains of battle at the foot of Mount Megiddo. John sees it as "great hailstones, heavy as a hundred weight [exactly what one would expect from such an earthquake and volcanic upheaval], dropped on men from heaven, till men cursed God for the plague of the hail, so fearful was that plague" (Revelation 16:21 RSV).

Man's madness, pride, and rebellion will destroy him. Even nature will war against him. In his sinful disobedience of God's commands upon his life, man has cursed the whole earth and he will eventually face his crime. Not even the elements of the universe can tolerate him forever in view of the way in which he has sought to destroy the equilibrium of the cosmos. There are certain inexorable laws of nature which cannot be disregarded without dire consequences. Thus man has created the conditions which will be his own undoing at the Battle of Armageddon.

The Sign of the Son of Man

This terrible battle, which culminates a series of uprisings during the entire seven years of Daniel's seventieth week, will be brought to its end by what Jesus calls "the sign of the Son of man in heaven" (Matthew 24:30). At the appearance of this sign all weapons will be turned in the direction of the heavens and every move will be concentrated on the new threat from the sky. This sign will appear at the moment of earthquakes, eruptions of the earth, and falling brimstone. And it will be the last straw.

Some have conjectured that the "sign of the Son of man" will be the "lightning" (24:27) which sets the skies aglow with a supernatural light similar to that which the shepherds saw on the night of the Messiah's birth (Luke 2:9). The sign of His First and Second Advent, according to this idea, would be one and the same. It has even been speculated that the sign will be that of the cross, such as Constantine saw and by which he was convinced of victory. There is no biblical hint of anything like this at all. We are safer to assume that the sign will be the appearance of Christ Himself as Daniel portrays His coming:

I saw in the night visions,
and behold, with the clouds of heaven

there came one like a son of man,
and he came to the Ancient of Days
and was presented before him.
And to him was given dominion
and glory and kingdom,
that all peoples, nations, and languages
should serve him;
his dominion is an everlasting dominion,
which shall not pass away,
and his kingdom one
that shall not be destroyed.

Daniel 7:13, 14 RSV

Jesus says that ". . . the tribes of the earth will mourn, and they will see the Son of man coming on the clouds of heaven with power and great glory" (Matthew 24:30 RSV). The wailing will be the nations' recognition of defeat in the divine sign which they have rejected. John sees that awesome moment: "Behold, he is coming with clouds, and every eye will see him, everyone who pierced him; and all tribes of the earth will wail on account of him . . ." (Revelation 1:7 RSV). There will be every reason to wail. The larger portion of the world's population will be finally destroyed.

The "wine press of the wrath of God" will be trodden and blood will flow "from the winepress, as high as a horse's bridle, for one thousand six hundred stadia" (14:20 RSV). The distance is about two hundred miles and covers the whole land of Israel. In the nineteenth chapter of the Apocalypse, John sees a terrible feasting on these slain bodies by the birds of the air. And there is little question but that this is what Jesus Himself was making reference to when He said to His disciples, in the midst of the discourse about the end of the age, "Wherever the carcass is, there the *vultures* will gather" (Matthew 24:28 LB). The land of Israel will be covered with carnage and the birds of prey will be sent to clean up the human pollution.

10
Come, Lord Jesus!

A Sight to Behold

That grand moment for which all history has waited may be just around the next turn of events. This present world order will not end with an act of man, but with the decisive movement of God. After the long night of rebellion and apostasy is over, the curtain will rise on the most glorious sight ever witnessed by mortal man. In a flash of holy brightness, like a thousand suns rolled into one, our Lord shall return in the clouds of heaven. Everyone alive on the earth after the devastation of Armageddon will see Him as visibly as did those first disciples watch His Ascension (Acts 1:11).

How all people will be able to view Him, since the world is round, has disturbed some who are bent on allowing God no secrets at all. Maybe it will be by some modern satellite-relayed television as has been suggested by technology-oriented minds. Certainly, the God who created all things will not be dependent on any mechanical device to be seen. The Lord has His own ways of communicating and He will surely have a simple method of making Himself visible to all the world at one and the same time.

Christ's coming will be a return to this earth in the same body as that which was seen and touched by the apostles during the interval between His Resurrection and Ascension (Matthew 28:9; Luke 24:31; John 20:-19, 29; 21:12). He will be no more a ghost at His return than He was when here among us the first time. Scripture is plain about the kind of bodily personage we may look for at the climax of the ages. Daniel foresaw "a Son of man" (Daniel 7:13) and Jesus spoke of His coming in human terms as well (Matthew 24:30; 26:64). He will not be essentially different in the world to come than He was when walking on this earth two thousand years ago. Our Lord shall still be "fully God and fully man" with no diminution of either facet of His being.

At the Ascension of our Lord, He was "crowned with glory and honor because of the suffering of death . . ." (Hebrews 2:9 RSV). And when He returns that is the way we shall see Him. John puts it like this: "We shall see him as he is" (1 John 3:2), which means that never again will Christ be seen as One despised and rejected. At His appearance we will see Him as the glorified Redeemer of all men and the King of kings promised to David himself. His coming will be in regal splendor and divine glory and all peoples shall bow before His power. In robes of righteousness and royalty our God shall appear to right the wrongs of all time and establish a totally new order of existence. History's yearning for redemption and fulfillment is to be realized in the returning Lord from heaven.

Accompanied by a Heavenly Entourage

If Antichrist is surrounded by fallen angels and demonic spirits (Revelation 16:13–16), Christ is accompanied by the hosts of heaven (19:14). Angels have always had a large part to play in the continuing war between good and evil. Since the fall of Satan prior to the creation of man this battle has been in progress. When the hour of judgment comes for men and women who are alive at the Second Coming, the Son of man will come ". . . in his glory, and all the angels with him" (Matthew 25:31). Presumably, this is the same angelic retinue as that of which Jesus spoke in the garden of Gethsemane when He rebuked Peter for the use of his sword: "Do you think that I cannot appeal to my Father, and he will at once send me more than twelve legions of angels?" (Matthew 26:53 RSV). Paul calls attention to the "mighty angels in flaming fire" (2Thessalonians 1:7 RSV) who will be with the Saviour at His revelation in the skies. Jude, brother of our Lord, quotes Enoch's prophecy, ". . . Behold, the Lord came with his holy myriads" (Jude 14 RSV).

These angels are to be used at the return of Christ to "gather his elect from the four winds, from one end of heaven to the other" (Matthew 24:31). It seems clear from the overall tenor of the biblical teaching relating to the end of the age that these heavenly beings are to be used like troops under the direct command of the King. Whatever the King demands, His heavenly troops will perform.

Another group of beings will also appear with Him at the Second Advent. Through the awful years of the tribulation the Church is to be with the Lord. The redeemed in Christ are caught up before the coming of Antichrist where they share in the marriage supper of the Lamb and receive their rewards for service rendered on earth during the Church age. The Lord of heaven will come *for* His Church at the time appointed and those who are *in Christ* by faith will be translated from this earth to the heavenly sphere. Therefore, when the Lord returns to the earth He will come *with* His saints who will share, as the Bride, in the glories of the Bridegroom. Zechariah envisions this truth in his early writings. In his vision of the Day of the Lord which was yet future, the prophet wrote, ". . . Then the Lord your God will come, and all the holy ones with him" (Zechariah 14:5 RSV). Paul promised the saints at Colossae, "When Christ who is our life appears, then you also will appear with him in glory" (Colossians 3:4 RSV).

To be allowed the joys of the eternal state is more than we can conceive. The thrill of being permitted to associate with the angels would be a blessing undeserved by any mortal man. But to be admitted into "the palace of the King" as His Bride forever is beyond our most fertile imagination! And yet, that is the relationship reserved for the Church for all eternity.

New Life for the Dead

To Mary and Martha Jesus had promised, "Your brother shall rise again" (John 11:23 RSV). Indeed, he did return from the dead where he had been for four days. As far as we know, however, Lazarus was later to be the victim of death as all men. The temporary conquest of death by Jesus in the life of this one man was a sign to the people of His day that someday the exception would become the rule for the children of God. Christ *is* "the resurrection and the life" and the man "who believes in [Him], though he die; yet shall he live" (11:25). On that glorious day of our Saviour's return to earth multitudes of people will share the new life which came to Lazarus. The difference is that it will be permanent for both him and all whose bodies await Christ's arrival.

It will not be forgotten that those who died in Christ between the crucifixion of Jesus and the translation of the Church will have been raised from the dead at the moment when the Lord returns for His Bride. But what is going to happen to those who accept Christ during the seven years and are killed by the Beast? Many shall seal their faith with their blood in response to the witnessing of the one hundred forty-four thousand and the two special witnesses whom God will send to announce the coming Kingdom. John saw ". . . a great multitude . . . standing before the throne and before the Lamb, clothed in white robes . . . and crying out with a loud voice, 'Salvation belongs to our God who sits upon the throne, and to the Lamb!' " (Revelation 7:9, 10 RSV). One of the elders identifies the multitudes as "they who have come out of great tribulation" (7:14). When are these saints to rise from their martyr graves?

Later, in the reference to the binding of Satan at the Second Coming of Christ, John says of those who had been beheaded by the Beast, ". . . They came to life, and reigned with Christ a thousand years" (20:4 RSV). This is a definite placing of the resurrection of the martyrs of the last prophetic week at the time of return of the Lord with His Bride. But still we have to do something with the saints of the Old Testament who were neither a part of the Church nor among the tribulation martyrs. Isaiah promised, "Thy dead shall live, their bodies shall rise. O dwellers in the dust, awake and sing for joy!" (Isaiah 26:19 RSV). But when? Daniel offers some help. In his prophecy about the time of the end, especially the last seven years, he writes, "And many of those who sleep in the dust of the earth shall awake, some to everlasting life . . ." (Daniel 12:2 RSV).

Obviously, on the basis of the biblical record, both the Old Testament saints and those who are martyred for resisting the Antichrist will be raised from the dead when the Saviour returns with the Church. Though separated from the rising from the grave of the deceased members of the Body of Christ at the translation by a period of seven years, this is still the *first* resurrection. The initial stage of this resurrection was the victory of Christ over death on the first day of the week. Second comes the translation of the Church with the rising of Christians from their places of bodily interment. Third is the resurrection of the Old Testament saints and the slain tribulation disciples at the return of Christ in judgment. All three of these stages are included in what John calls "the first resurrection" (Revelation 20:5) since *first* suggests "something before" that which follows. The second resurrection ("second death"—20.6) is reserved for the wicked while the first includes only the righteous. Therefore, the three phases are all to be seen as distinct acts of God *in time*, but only one *in kind*.

Judgment Comes to Israel

As last minute preparations are made for the realization of the Davidic Kingdom as a pure theocracy, the Jews will be called together to determine who shall be permitted admittance into the thousand years of peace. The scene is pictured for us by the prophet Ezekiel.

> I will bring you out from the peoples and gather you out from the countries where you are scattered, with a mighty hand and an outstretched arm, and with wrath poured out; and I will bring you into the wilderness of the peoples, and there I will enter with your fathers in the wilderness of the land of Egypt, so I will enter into judgment with you, says the Lord God. I will make you pass under the rod, and will let you go in by number. I will purge out the rebels from among you, and those who transgress against me; I will bring them out of the land where they sojourn, but they shall not enter the land of Israel . . . .
>
> Ezekiel 20:34–38 RSV

The company of Jews included in these words is made up of those who manage to escape the scourge of the Antichrist against them and the horrors of the great battle. Also, Jews from all over the world will be gathered in Palestine to be judged. Paul writes to the Gentile Romans that "all Israel shall be saved" (Romans 11:26), but earlier in the letter he has enunciated the truth that "not all who are descended from Israel belong to Israel, and not all are children of Abraham because they are his descendants . . ." (9:6,7). What this verifies is that all who are a part of the true Israel by faith in the Messiah and His Kingdom will be granted entrance into the theocratic reign. By the same token, being a Jew in the flesh alone is insufficient reason for such acceptance.

Some of the peoples in the new State of Israel will have accepted their coming Kingdom and its King during the tribulation and escaped death. Their kind will be saved. And while it is their faith which saves them, their works are important enough to be surveyed and examined by the Judge.

> "Then I will draw near to you for judgment; I will be a swift witness against the sorcerers, against the adulterers, against those who swear falsely, against those who oppress the hireling in his wages, the widow and the orphan, against those who thrust aside the sojourner, and do not fear me," says the Lord of hosts.
>
> Malachi 3:5 RSV

Deeds are included in the criteria for judging, not because any will be saved by works, but because one's works grow out of his faith and thus prove it. Abraham himself was saved by faith (Hebrews 11:8–10).

As they watched Him ascend from the Mount of Olives, the believing Jewish apostles were promised that their Lord would come back in the same way they had watched Him depart. The interlude of the Church age stopped the prophetic clock. When Jesus comes back for His Church the clock will begin ticking off the last minutes of the world order as we know it. And at that moment when He comes in judgment to establish the Kingdom of Israel as promised to the patriarchs, the King will begin at the precise point from which he took leave. Listen to the prophet of twenty-five hundred years ago explaining how it will happen.

> On that day his [the coming Christ] feet shall stand on the Mount of Olives which lies before Jerusalem on the east; and the Mount of Olives shall be split in two from east to west by a very wide valley; so that one-half of the Mount shall withdraw northward, and the other half southward.
>
> Zechariah 14:4

Known to all Bible students is the fact that the Mount of Olives has two high spots between which exists a fault or weakness which probably traces the path of the coming cataclysmic break when the Lord's feet stand again at the place from which He ascended. It is here that the judgment will take place. And it is from this sacred Mount that Christ will restore the Kingdom to Israel.

A Day of Reckoning for the Nations

Our most graphic portrayal of the Lord as returning Judge is given to us by the most apocalyptic of Jesus' apostles. No longer does he see Jesus on a donkey in humiliation, but he envisions Him on a white charger riding in victory. His word picture is so well done that one must let him speak for himself.

> Then I saw heaven opened, and behold a white horse! He who sat upon it is called Faithful and True, and in righteousness he judges and makes war. His eyes are like a flame of fire, and on his head are many diadems; and he has a name inscribed which no one knows but himself. He is clad in a robe dipped in blood, and the name by which he is called is The Word of God. And the armies of heaven, arrayed in fine linen, white and pure, followed him on white horses. From his mouth issues a sharp sword with which to smite the nations, and he will rule them with a rod of iron; he will tread the wine press of the fury of the wrath of God the Almighty. On his robe and on his thigh he has a name inscribed, King of kings and Lord of lords.
>
> Revelation 19:11–16

It is manifest that the judgment in this passage is meted out to the Gentiles. Specifically "the nations" are mentioned which makes the point clear. Furthermore, there is no question as to who the Judge is since John calls Him "The Word of God," the name given by the same author, in the prologue to his gospel, to the articulated Being of God incarnate in human flesh (John 1:1–14).

None can overlook the effort of Antichrist to imitate the One on "a white horse" at the outset of the last prophetic week (Revelation 6:2).

The rider on the earlier white charger came promising peace while thrusting the world into war. The Rider on the latter horse comes in declared judgment in order to bring universal peace at last. The "sharp sword" with which He "smites the nations" is seen coming from His mouth. The psalmist speaks of men whose tongues are "a sharp sword" (Psalm 57:4). By that he means that their words are cutting and destructive. Likewise, the writer of Proverbs says that God's word is "sharp as a two-edged sword" (Proverbs 5:4 RSV). No further insight is needed to convince us that the instrument of judgment and destruction upon the wicked is *The Word of God* Himself! Luther had this in mind when he convincingly sang of Christ's final confrontation with Satan, "One little word shall fell him." It is that divine Word which called all things into being which will also inflict judgment upon evil in its every form.

Although it is abundantly true (with the Gentiles as it is with the Jews) that man will be saved by faith alone, his works have a way of expressing tangibly what his faith actually is. No one more aptly captures this truth than James: "So faith by itself, if it has no works, is dead. . . . I by my works will show you my faith" (James 2:17, 18 RSV). Those Gentile works, which will best reveal the hearts of non-Jews toward Christ as they have lived through the tribulation, are described for us in the Master's words as recorded by Matthew. Christ is pictured sitting on His throne with the nations (Gentiles) before Him. A separation is taking place between the sheep and the goats—the sheep on the right hand of the Shepherd-King and the goats on the left. To those who are accepted by the One on the throne, the Lord explains,

> For I was hungry and you gave me food, I was thirsty and you gave me drink, I was a stranger and you welcomed me, I was naked and you clothed me, I was sick and you visited me, I was in prison and you came to me. . . . Truly, I say to you, as you did it to one of the least of these my brethren, you did it to me.
>
> Matthew 25:35, 36, 40 RSV

Gentiles who are rejected from admission to the reign of peace are those who failed in the kind of life for which the faithful are commended in the above words.

Who are the Lord's "brethren"? They are the Jews! No one could possibly fail to understand that if he has read the Scriptures at all carefully. Thus, Jesus is insisting that one's attitude toward the Hebrew people has an eternal bearing on his acceptance or rejection by God. Four thousand years ago, God assured Abraham and his descendants that the nations would "bless themselves" or be cursed by the way they treat the chosen people. Nations, as a whole, who have vigorously oppressed the Jews have suffered for it. And someday, individuals will be received into the Kingdom's reign or expelled from the presence of the Lord on the basis of their attitude toward the Israelites. This will especially be so of those who live through the tribulation period. In light of this we can better understand the strong dedication of certain persons who spend their entire lives as missionaries to the Jews. There is no finer way to fulfill the Lord's plan for the Jewish people than by pointing them to their Messiah, even Christ the King.

But Gentiles and Jews, who have not turned to the Lord as Saviour and proved their faith by their service to God and their attitude toward the Kingdom, will be slain "by the sword of him who sits upon the horse, the sword that issues from his mouth . . ." (Revelation 19:21 RSV). In no way should we allow ourselves to think of our Lord as being vicious or even harsh because of this warlike appearance. As has been pointed out, the sword is symbolic for the Word of God. Shortly before the cross, Jesus warned us about this day of judgment.

If any man hear my words, and believe not, I judge him not: for I came not to judge the world, but to save the world. He that rejecteth me, and receiveth not my words, hath one that judgeth him: the word that I have spoken, the same shall judge him in the last day.

John 12:47, 48

Nothing could be clearer. No man is left in the dark about what is to come. The same Word which brings life when accepted brings death if spurned. "The word of God is quick, and powerful, and sharper than any two-edged sword . . ." (Hebrews 4:12).

Sentencing of the Beasts

In the concluding moments of the Battle of Armageddon, the Antichrist and his confederation of vassal kings are scheduled to attack the returning Son of God. Manifestly, their carnal weapons have no power over Him who long ago conquered death and is "alive for evermore" (Revelation 1:18). Nevertheless, the attempt on His life will be made. What follows cannot be called a battle in the ordinary use of that word. Tersely the account is given: "They will make war on the Lamb, and the Lamb shall overcome them, for he is Lord of lords and King of kings, and they that are with him are called and chosen and faithful" (17:14). How the Lamb will overcome the Beast is not told us in detail. We are only guaranteed that such will be the outcome of the agelong conflict between the forces of good and evil.

The Apostle to the Gentiles has a word about the manner in which the Beast will be overcome, a suggestion fully in line with what would be expected in light of Christ's judgment on Jews and Gentiles alike. Of the Antichrist, Paul says, ". . . the Lord Jesus will slay him with the breath of his mouth and destroy him by his appearing and his coming" (2 Thessalonians 2:8 RSV). Here again is a reference to the use of the Word of God as a weapon of destruction when it has been flouted and spurned. Little difference exists between the "sword of his mouth" and the "breath of his mouth." In these words one can sense that it is the eternal Word of Jehovah which brings about the ultimate downfall of the Antichrist.

An additional point of interest is provided in the term "captured" to describe the handling of both the Beast and the false prophet (Revelation 19:20). Military language is employed throughout the Apocalypse. Probably we are to perceive this term as a symbol of the submission of both the political and ecclesiastical power to the immutable and unconquerable Word. When one is captured he cannot help himself. Under such circumstances he absolutely is incapable of further resistance. Nothing is left for him but unconditional surrender. Indubitably, the divine Word will have the final authority.

Once the Beast and the false prophet are brought into submission to "the breath of his mouth" they are both "cast alive into the lake of fire burning with brimstone" (19:20). It will be recalled that brimstone can be likened to the red-hot pitch which rained down on Sodom, the wicked city of the plains in Abraham's day. In the Old Testament, the place where Christ casts the Beast and his co-worker is called *Topheth*, "a place of burning" (cf. Isaiah 30:33). This is not *Hades* (abode of the wicked dead), a temporary prison until the time of the White Throne Judgment. This is *hell*, symbolized by Jesus as the burning dumping ground outside the city of Jerusalem (Mark 9:43–48). The fires will be stoked and ready for their first two victims. Whether the fires are literal or not is beside the point. The torment of *hell* will be far worse than fire alone could ever be. And it will be forever.

Satan in a Holding Pattern

Lucifer did his damage in heaven and he has ceaselessly "caused havoc" upon the earth. For the last half of the tribulation period his efforts will be greatly intensified as we have seen in an earlier section of our study. His two colleagues in evil—Antichrist and the false prophet —having been cast into *hell*, Satan will be dealt with next in the solution to the problem of evil as determined by God at the beginning of the human race. He who has been responsible for all the wickedness and heartache since the fall of Adam is to be consigned to a place of stringent restriction from which he will not be permitted to make further attacks upon the earth. His days of manipulation will be passed and his contacts shall be confined to the world of evil spirits (Jude 6). John succinctly depicts the event like this:

> Then I saw an angel coming down from heaven, holding in his hand the key of the bottomless pit and a great chain. And he seized the dragon, that ancient serpent, who is the Devil and Satan, and bound him for a thousand years, and threw him into the pit, and shut it and sealed it over him, that he should deceive the nations no more, till the thousand years were ended. . . .
>
> Revelation 20:1–3 RSV

With the use of the Greek term *abussos*, rendered "bottomless pit," one discovers that Satan is not cast into the same place as the Antichrist and his false prophet. They are to be in *hell* permanently, but Satan is in the *pit* for one thousand years. He is not destroyed, only defeated and taken captive by the Lord Jesus Christ. His being bound with a chain emphatically affirms the sovereignty of God over His number one enemy. The pit, or abyss, is the dwelling place of the evil spirits. It is from this area of dark and foul demons that the devil marshalls his vast army to defy God, seduce man, and defeat Christ. At last he will be shut up in his own quarters, however, where he will have a thousand years to design a new strategy for his last invasion of the Kingdom of God. It is during this millennium of the imprisonment of Satan that the Appointed Heir to David's throne will rule in peace and righteousness over the whole earth. In the next chapter we shall look at that joyous and exciting reign of the King of kings.

11
The Dawn of the Kingdom of God

What God Has Wrought!

Can any of us even faintly conceive what the incredible blessings of a world under the direct rule of God, without the interference of Satan, shall be like? Surely, there will be great and wonderful surprises beyond our dreams. Yet, God has given us some insight in the Scriptures. He has even further granted us spiritual perception by which we just sense some things "in our bones." Paul felt this tingle up his spine as he penned those oft-quoted words, "What no eye has seen, nor ear heard, nor the heart of man conceived, what God has prepared for those who love him [quoted from Isaiah 64:4], God has revealed to us through the Spirit . . ." (1 Corinthians 2:9, 10 RSV). In a very special way, that is true as regards our premonitions about the life to be in the Millennium.

For thousands of years man has been trying to create a paradise out of the earth. Since the moment of Adam's rebellion which brought a curse upon every part of God's creation, conditions have grown worse. At certain intervals in the long trek from primitive to modern man a ray of hope has broken through and humanity predicted better things for itself. In every instance it has been the inevitable plight of the human race to slip back into its old patterns and render its gains of no lasting significance. Hence, in our technological culture of the last half of the twentieth century, we are confronted with a world filled with evil and its damning results. Everywhere we are seeing and hearing about the determination of modern man to do away with war, poverty, and injustice. The facts do not indicate that we are being successful. Poverty is increasing, prejudice and discrimination are growing, and war seems inevitable. We have made a giant-size mess out of God's world.

By now many people are beginning to suspect that the world's only hope must come from outside man himself. Even those who have no such proneness towards a recognition of the supernatural are bemoaning the hopeless fate of the human race. A few still cling to man's *innate goodness* with blinkers on their eyes and argue that mortal man will yet produce an earthly utopia; but their numbers are rapidly decreasing. Regardless of what men may think or say we have been assured by the prophets, the apostles, and Jesus Himself that God will finally step into the cosmic dilemma and set everything right. There is no biblical word more dogmatically affirmed than that.

An Original Plan Realized

When the Creator placed man in the primeval garden it was the immediate plan of the divine Spirit to establish an unbroken relationship between Himself and man by which the creature would live in peace and prosperity all his days. Falling into disobedience almost at once, man forced God to postpone the design for man into the future. The selection of one man to obediently found a Kingdom in the midst of the idolatrous descendants of Adam was a part of that long-range plan. When the people of Abraham failed in their share of the covenant the Lord turned their existence into one prolonged period of discipline. In the interval, He called out a distinct group from the world who would enjoy a favored place in the world to come. That place would be granted purely on the basis of the commitment made by those people to Christ in faith. In time, God's plans include another round with the chosen people of the Kingdom which floundered on the shoals of disobedience. And at that time the originally designed Kingdom of God will be established and finally the whole universe shall again become a paradise of the Creative Spirit. The original plan will be realized.

This has to be so lest God and His Christ are a failure. The Creator did not start something which He cannot finish. Christ is "the Alpha and Omega, the beginning and the ending . . ." (Revelation 1:8). What has been intended by a sovereign Trinity shall be culminated exactly as the Godhead wills. Not one *i* will be left without a dot nor will a single *t* be uncrossed. Although it has been a long time in coming, the promised Kingdom shall arrive. Our Saviour promised this fulfillment of the divine plan even as He faced the cross. Holding in His hands the cup which symbolized His own blood, He said, "Truly I say unto you, I shall not drink again of the fruit of the vine until that day when I drink it new in the kingdom of God" (Mark 14:25 RSV). None of the disciples fully perceived all that was wrapped up in that statement of prophecy, but not a single man misconstrued what was meant by the Kingdom yet to come.

Daniel interpreted King Nebuchadnezzar's dream in which the king had seen an image with frightening appearance but which was smote by a stone and destroyed. The explanation of the dream was a prophetic picture of the kingdoms of Babylon, Medo-Persia, Greece, and Rome. The latter kingdom was represented by "feet partly of iron and partly of clay" and the mountain stone, which "was cut by no human hand," struck those vulnerable feet of the image and destroyed it completely. The stone was unquestionably the Messiah and it "became a great mountain and filled the whole earth." In conclusion, the prophet exclaimed, "The dream is certain and its interpretation sure" (Daniel 2:31–45 RSV). No fact is more certain than that "the earth shall be full of the knowledge of the Lord as the waters cover the sea" (Isaiah 11:9 RSV).

Eden Improved

John Milton talked about paradise *lost* and paradise *regained*. Everyone knows that we have lost it but not everyone is aware that it can be found again. The kind of life which Adam and Eve enjoyed in the garden before their sin is a sample of what the earth will be like during the reign of Christ on the throne of David. Moses describes conditions prior to the fall in the loveliest of words:

The Lord God planted a garden in Eden, to the east, and placed in the garden the man he had formed. The Lord God planted all sorts of beautiful trees there in the garden, trees producing the choicest of fruit. At the center of the garden he placed the Tree of Life, and also the Tree of Conscience, giving knowledge of Good and Bad. A river from the land of Eden flowed through the garden to water it; afterwards the river divided into four branches. One of these was named the Pishon; it winds across the entire length of the land of Havilah, where nuggets of pure gold are found, also beautiful bdellium and even lapis lazuli. The second branch is called the Gihon, crossing the entire length of the land of Cush, the third branch is the Tigris, which flows to the east of the city of Asher. And the fourth is the Euphrates.

Genesis 2:8–14 LB

One can envision a perfect land where everything is beautiful and good and where there is nothing to disturb or molest the peaceful pursuit of personal fulfillment in the presence of God.

In portraying the coming of the Messiah to the Mount of Olives, Zechariah mentions the intriguing fact that "on that day living waters shall flow out from Jerusalem, half of them to the eastern sea, and half of them to the western sea; it shall continue in summer as in winter" (Zechariah 14:8 RSV). Even the waters of Eden will be brought to the Holy City where, at the present time, there is no river at all! An even more exciting prediction about these health-giving waters, free from pollution, is given by Ezekiel (47:1-12). Palestine is located at the approximate center of the world's continents and it is understandable why the healing waters should emanate from that point in the Millennium. Accompanying the fresh waters will be a renewed earth and air so that the soil will become abundantly productive (cf. Amos 9:13, 14; Zechariah 3:10; 8:12; Isaiah 55:13; 41:18, 19; Romans 8:19-22).

With the population problem corrected by the overwhelming reduction in people from the earth, man's life will be greatly extended so that, except in rare instances of open rebellion, he will live a thousand years if on the earth at the beginning of the millennial reign—longer than Methuselah! This should not surprise us when it is remembered that the One who brought healing and strength to the diseased and infirm while on the earth the first time, will be present again to make wholeness as natural as brokenness has been. Isaish sees the time:

> . . . the eyes of the blind shall be opened,
> and the ears of the deaf unstopped;

then shall the lame man leap like a hart,
and the tongue of the dumb sing for joy.
For waters shall break forth in the wilderness,
and streams in the desert.

Isaiah 35:5, 6

Still there is more. The regained paradise will be even better than the original Eden. The Tree of Conscience will still be here so that it is *possible* to sin, but Satan himself will not be around. To live in the Garden of Eden without the tempter is the utopia which humankind has sought so long without success. And that is due to the unavoidable influence of the devil which is now everywhere man goes and a part of all his endeavors. Utopia is God's gift to the faithful. It is never man's gift to himself. Of God's making is the Kingdom and it will come when He binds Satan and places on David's throne Him "to whom it belongs" (Genesis 49:10 RSV).

Righteousness and Peace at Last

Mankind has tried every conceivable form of human government. Some have been better than others but they have all had the germs of evil decay at heart. It is not long before any new approach to governing people starts to deteriorate. This is so because both the governed and the governors are sinful by nature. God has the only perfect system. We call it a *theocracy*—the ruling of man by the will of God. And this is the kind of rule we will have when Christ is on David's throne. "For the Lord of hosts will reign on Mount Zion and in Jerusalem . . ." (Isaiah 24:23 RSV) and His "people will abide in a peaceful habitation, in secure dwellings, and in quiet resting places" (32:18 RSV).

The injustice of which men have complained since the genesis of time shall be corrected for Christ "will rule them with a rod of iron" (Revelation 19:15). Selfishness, under the disguise of a struggle for justice, will be exposed. Men will live together in righteousness and peace when He who has been at the right hand of the Father sits on His rightful throne —and the enemies of the Kingdom are "made his footstool" (Hebrews 10:13). "He shall reign for ever and ever" (Revelation 11:15) "for he must reign till he hath put all enemies under his feet" (1 Corinthians

15:25). Zechariah's prophecy will be brought to pass in its entirety when "the battle bow shall be cut off, and he shall command peace to the nations . . ." (Zechariah 9:10 RSV).

No more will hostility and fear fill the air. It is not enough to say that men will live in peace, but we must also point out that the animal kingdom in its entirety will exist in harmony. The Messianic prophet *par excellence* says it this way:

> The wolf shall dwell with the lamb,
>   and the leopard shall lie down with the kid,
> and the calf and the lion and the fatling together,
>   and a little child shall lead them.
> The cow and the bear shall feed;
>   their young shall lie down together;
>   and the lion shall eat straw like the ox.
> The sucking child shall play over the hole of the asp,
>   and the weaned child shall put his hand on the adder's den.
>   Isaiah 11:6–8 RSV (cf. Ezekiel 34:25)

In this description of the Millennium we see restored the relationship between man and the beasts which characterized the Garden of Eden.

At last the prophecy which points to a time when there will be no more wars will be realized. A common mistake made by persons and groups seeking peace for the nations in a sinful world is to quote Isaiah's prophecy as though it can be fulfilled before the coming of the Lord. There is no way to have world peace until the Prince of peace has returned to sit on the promised throne. Then, and only then, shall nations "beat their swords into plowshares, and their spears into pruninghooks . . ." (Isaiah 2:4). Until that day the reverse pattern will be true: We will "beat . . . plowshares into swords, and . . . pruninghooks into spears" (Joel 3:10). It is easy to see that the latter prophecy alone has come true in this present world order—the kingdom of man.

A Chance for Everyone

Men and women who survive the tribulation and gain entrance into the millennial reign with Christ will still be as human as ever. They will retain their mortal bodies and will live in families and have children. The charter members of the Kingdom will all be in complete accord with the will of Christ. Then shall come to pass that promise made by Paul to the Philippians that ". . . at the name of Jesus every knee should bow, in heaven and on earth and under the earth, and every tongue confess that Jesus Christ is Lord, to the glory of God the Father" (Philippians 2:10,11 RSV). As children are born, however, who do not know of the way things were before the Son of God sat on the throne in Jerusalem, the fallen nature of humankind will begin to exert itself. For this reason the King will rule with a hand of iron. There may be an occasional attempt at rebellion but, if such should be the case, the King of Righteousness will immediately put an end to it. With the glorified Church reigning with Him and the heavenly hosts serving as His defenders of state, the world will experience the kind of *good dictatorship* it desired in its deceived worship of the Antichrist.

Across the thousand years there will be growing numbers of new people who will, on the basis of human nature, be possessed with a selfish discontent. Even with the Lord Himself on the throne, they will feel that things could be better if they themselves were in control. Multitudes will be redeemed by faith in the Saviour-King through the witnessing of faithful Jews—but not all. No one will be admitted into the eternal dimension at the end of the Millennium unless he had accepted the Redeemer for himself. Therefore, after the thousand years of peace, God will offer the unrepentant the chance to choose whom they will serve—not because His hand is iron and compelling, but because they love and accept Him as Saviour and Lord.

It must not be overlooked that conditions will be totally reversed during the Millennium in so far as evangelism is concerned. For the interval of the Church age it has been the Gentiles who were commissioned to lead the world to Christ. To be sure, Jesus' Great Commission was given to His disciples, all of whom were Jews, but the task soon became the responsibility of the Gentiles since the Jews gradually rebelled against the new faith. Granted, not nearly enough has been done to convert the Jews, but the initiative which we have seen has been taken by Gentile Christians. In the Millennium it will be the Jews, converted during the seven years of tribulation, who will evangelize the nations.

And they will be widely successful. One of the prophets, to whom we have made regular reference, foresees it like this:

> In those days ten men from the nations of every tongue shall take hold of the robe of a Jew, saying, "Let us go with you, for we have heard that God is with you."
>
> Zechariah 8:23 RSV.

Isaiah just as excitedly pictures the future glory of Zion and the spread of the righteousness of the Kingdom when he writes,

> And nations shall come to your light,
>   and kings to the brightness of your rising.
>
> Lift up your eyes round about, and see;
>   they all gather together, they come to you;
> your sons shall come from far,
>   and your daughters shall be carried in the arms.
>
> Isaiah 60:3, 4 RSV

> . . . They shall declare my glory among the nations.
>
> 66:19 RSV

Nonetheless, in spite of the evangelistic success of the Jews, many will not give glory to the King of their own volition. Their obedience will be given because He is strong and an overthrow of His righteous government is impossible.

Satan Has His Last Fling

Lest unredeemed men and women in the millennial period be able to say that they had no chance to express their true wills, a brief time will be arranged at the close of the thousand years for just such personal expression. Although the people shall have lived under a perfectly just and righteous system of government, there are many who will revolt against the King at that time. Their cry will still be, "We will not have this man to rule over us." Thus, the depravity of human nature is going to be seen stripped bare of any pretense when man can proudly challenge the gracious rule of the Lord Himself after the varied benefits of His love enjoyed by all. Furthermore, it will be plain for all to see that man's nature can never be changed with anything less than an inner transformation of heart motive by the acceptance of Christ as Lord and Saviour.

Giving them the opportunity to choose between Himself and His sworn enemy, God will release Satan from the pit where he has been bound throughout the Millennium. John tells us the way it will happen.

> When the thousand years end, Satan will be let out of his prison. He will go out to deceive the nations of the world and gather them together, with Gog and Magog, for battle—a mighty host, numberless as sand along the shore. They will go up across the broad plain of the earth and surround God's people and the beloved city of Jerusalem on every side. . . .
>
> Revelation 20:7–9 LB

At the time of the exodus of the devil from his pit of confinement, great hordes of people who have never been tempted before, will be seduced into a participation in an uprising against the King on David's throne. These people will come from all over the earth, not just from the old northern kingdom of Gog which was devastated by God in its invasion of Israel early in the last prophetic week. The reference here to Gog and Magog indicates that the objective of the peoples will be the same, but the result will be a repeat performance of what happened to Russia— still remembered by some even after a thousand years! Gog and Magog, at that time, will have become a byword for defeat.

The attack is to be made directly on "the beloved city of Jerusalem." Again, all the power of evil is said to be hurled against the one spot on earth where righteousness and truth is concentrated. To conquer that city would be to overthrow David's throne, capture the King, and win in the age-old conflict between God and Lucifer. Every citizen of the millennial era is to be given the choice to accept Christ and live forever in the eternal state to follow or to choose Satan's way and spend eternity in hell. The fact that many will choose to cast their lot with the Evil

One will prove once and for all that not even the most perfect conditions and the most excellent environment of a whole millennium will suffice to change man's heart. Nothing can ever alter the nature of man except an inner relationship with the living Christ by saving faith in His person and work.

After a thousand years the Antichrist and the false prophet are still seen in "the lake of fire" awaiting the arrival of the next occupant. Hell is everlasting retribution and there is no escape from it ever! The fire of heaven, like that which fell on Sodom, will consume the armies of Satan as they come against Jerusalem. Then God shall deal with the devil in ultimate judgment. He will "be thrown into the Lake of Fire burning with sulphur where the Creature and False Prophet are, and they will be tormented day and night forever and ever" (Revelation 20:10 LB). At last the scourge of all time will be everlastingly punished. His cause will be irremediably lost. And the righteous will stand at the threshold of everlasting joy and peace.

One word should be said at this point about the wicked angels, the demonic spirits who have served Satan so well in his influence and possession of men's minds and bodies. Of these fallen angels Jude writes, "The angels that did not keep their own position but left their proper dwelling have been kept by him in eternal chains in the nether gloom until the judgment of the great day" (Jude 6 RSV). Simon Peter makes mention of this same pit-dwelling of the wicked angels until the judgment (2 Peter 2:4). And when Jesus gives His discourse on the future of the nations, He states that this "eternal fire" has been "prepared for the devil and his angels" (Matthew 25:41 RSV). Thus, it is rather clear that the Beast and false prophet will be the first to suffer the torments of hell, the devil and his demonic company to follow after one thousand years. This will be the beginning of the divine solution to the problem of pollution since all contamination on the earth has its source in the work of Satan.

At the Bar of the Supreme Court

One thing remains to be done after the "devil and his angels" are cast into hell. It is commonly known as the Great White Throne Judgment.

The definitive title comes from the Apocalypse itself: "Then I saw a great white throne and him who sat upon it; from his presence earth and sky fled away, and no place was found for them" (Revelation 20:11 RSV). This is not "the judgment seat of Christ" where the saints have received their rewards. Neither is this "the judgment of the nations" at the end of the great tribulation. This is the *final judgment* upon the wicked dead from the beginning of the human race until the end of the Millennium. Already we have discussed the first resurrection. The second resurrection takes place a thousand years after the first. It is a resurrection unto eternal death. Of this event John writes,

> The rest of the dead did not come to life until the thousand years were ended. . . .Blessed and holy is he who shares in the first resurrection! Over such the second death has no power. . . . And I saw the dead, great and small, standing before the throne, and the books were opened. Also another book was opened, which is the book of life. And the dead were judged by what was written in the books, by what they had done. And the sea gave up the dead in it, Death and Hades gave up the dead in them, and all were judged by what they had done.
>
> Revelation 20:5, 6, 12, 13 RSV

Jesus warned the people that "the hour is coming when all who are in the tombs will hear his voice and come forth, those who have done good, to the resurrection of life, and those who have done evil, to the resurrection of judgment" (John 5:28, 29 RSV). Paul is certain ". . . that there will be a resurrection of both the just and the unjust" (Acts 24:15). The presence of the "book of life" at this final judgment is conclusive proof that the dead called forth from the grave (whether in the earth or the sea) are lost due to their failure to accept Christ as Saviour. *Hades*, where they had been awaiting the time of the judgment, was its own guarantee of lostness. The use of "the books" infers that the *levels* of punishment are determined on the basis of works.

> Then Death and Hades were thrown into the lake of fire. This is the second death, the lake of fire; and if any one's name was not

found written in the book of life, he was thrown into the lake of
fire.

Revelation 20:14, 15 RSV

At this juncture in the program of divine events, hell will be overpopulated! With the harvest of the wicked of all the ages, Hell is said
to be a place where "there shall be weeping and gnashing of teeth"
(Matthew 8:12; 22:13; 24:51; 25:30; Luke 13:28). Such a condition
suggests deplorable conditions of an unbearable proximity. And while
hell becomes overpopulated (that fate is a part of the punishment), the
population problem on the earth will be solved at last.

An End to Pollution

Long ago the princely prophet looked forward to a time when the
world would be purified of everything which has interfered with the
beauty, peace, and harmony designed by the Creator. He heard God
saying:

> For behold, I create new heavens
> and a new earth;
> and the former things shall not be remembered
> or come into mind.

Isaiah 65:17 RSV

John gives us a radiant picture of what that new realm will be like
(Revelation 21:1–22:5). But the one New Testament penman who explains how it will happen is Saint Peter.

> The day of the Lord is surely coming, as unexpectedly as a thief,
> and then the heavens will pass away with a terrible noise and the
> heavenly bodies will disappear in fire, and the earth and everything
> on it will be burned up. . . . You should look forward to that day
> and hurry it along—the day when God will set the heavens on fire,
> and the heavenly bodies will melt and disappear in flames. But we
> are looking forward to God's promise of new heavens and a new

earth afterwards, where there will be only goodness.

                              2 Peter 3:10, 12, 13 LB

By these words we are not to assume that Peter means annihilation. Not one bit of matter which God has made will ever be done away. The conflagration which is here depicted will change the form of matter, but not annihilate it. Nothing God has ever made will be deprived of existence. It may disappear from the natural eye, be transformed into gas or energy, but it does not cease to be. Man himself lives forever somewhere in some changed condition. Hell does not do away with man any more than heaven puts an end to him. Likewise, the universe was made by God and nothing good will be annihilated. But it will be changed from the global matter which we now know into a new form of habitable existence. Certainly, "the new heavens and the new earth" will be conducive to the kind of bodies the saints of God will receive in the world to come.

If one is concerned about the state of the people of God during this terrible holocaust, let it be noted that God protected the three Hebrew children from the fiery blast even within the furnace of Nebuchadnezzar! If He could do it then, He can do it again. Furthermore, there is something indestructible about righteousness. It lives on through the fire.

Plainly the Scriptures teach us that everything that defiles or pollutes will be burnt out of the universe. Sin's contamination will be gone forever. The pollutants which have alarmed us of late are destined for the divine fire. One day the heavens are going to be cleared of all which now makes the atmosphere a risk to breathe. The waters will be purified and life will abound within them. With all the contaminants of the soil gone, the earth will be totally free of its curse and man will live in harmony with it as did Adam before his sin. God hates pollution. He has promised to deal with it. And He will! In the next chapter we shall see some of the renovated splendor which may be expected in the life that shall one day become a blessed reality to the people of the Lord.

12
A Renewed World—God's Solution

The Newness of the Earth

From the creation of "the heavens and the earth" (Genesis 1:1) to the creation of "a new heaven and a new earth" (Revelation 21:1) all existence has been restricted to a space-time continuum. Before the universe came into being at the Word of God there was no space nor was there any time. This is what is called *eternity*. Following the conflagration, which will purify the cosmos at the end of the age, all being will return to the antecreation state. That is, space and time as we have known it will be no more. Eternity is going to be spaceless (in the sense of unlimited) and timeless (in the sense of unending). Our present world order has been an interval or parenthesis between these two eternities.

The new earth will have been fully cleansed by the purgating fires of the Creator Himself. Everything will have the distinct look and feel of newness and freshness about it. Assuredly, there will still be points of recognition even as Jesus' resurrection body was identifiable by the disciples. Yet, in the same manner in which those disciples found the Master's appearance splendidly different, so the earth is to be reformed by God.

Those surprises which await us in the world to come are bound to be far more exciting and eternally exhilarating than anyone can describe with his human vocabulary. John has this universal problem in trying to draw word pictures of what he saw in his vision. When he talks about gold streets, pearly gates, gem-studded walls, and inexhaustible light, it is obvious that he is desperately seeking to depict an eternal glory with the best analogies available. We almost sense the apostle's frustration in being unable to find the words which will really convey the unutterable beauty of the new earth.

One of the first observations made by the seer is that "the sea was no more" (Revelation 21:1). The seas have always been symbolic of separation and loneliness. It is the vast bodies of water which divide the continents and peoples of the earth. When one recalls that John was on an island away from the mainland where was his beloved Ephesus, the feeling of being shut out and alone is greatly heightened. Apparently, the oceans with their pollution are to be no more. Renewed humanity will have nothing to divide man from man. The only source of water will be "the river of the water of life, bright as crystal, flowing from the throne of God and of the Lamb" (22:1 RSV). And it is to be as uncontaminated as is the nature of the God who sits on the throne from which it issues. Like the river which "flowed out of Eden to water the garden" (Genesis 2:10), the heavenly river will bring health and healing to all. "To the thirsty," says the Lord, ". . . I will give water without price from the fountain of the water of life" (Revelation 21:6 RSV).

Even the Heavens Are New

It seems that the new heavens will be without sun, moon, or stars. A connection may be found here between the ancient tendency to worship the celestial hosts (as well as the modern affinity for sun-worship) and the ultimate disappearance of any substitute for the living God. Numbers of prophecies suggest that something is going to happen to the heavenly luminaries in the coming world. Joel says that in the latter days "the sun and the moon shall be dark, and the stars shall withdraw their shining" (Joel 2:10; 3:15). In his prophecy regarding the Messianic Kingdom and the troublous days which accompany it (which word Peter insists was partially fulfilled at Pentecost—Acts 2:17–21), Joel is specific: "The sun shall be turned to darkness, and the moon into blood, before the great and terrible day of the Lord come" (Joel 2:31).

Our Lord speaks of the same fate for the shining hosts of heaven in His warning related to the *parousia* of the Son of man: "After the tribulation of those days the sun will be darkened, and the moon will not give its light, and the stars will fall from heaven, and the powers of the heavens will be shaken" (Matthew 24:29; cf. Mark 13:24; Luke 23:45). In the beginning of the created order God dispelled the darkness of the formless deep through an act by which the transcendent Creator became immanent in His creation. "Let there be light," said God, "and there was light. And God saw that the light was good; and God separated the light from the darkness" (Genesis 1:3, 4 RSV). Clearly we see that there was light long before the appearance of the "lights in the firmament of the heavens" (1:14 RSV). The sun, moon, and stars were not formed until the fourth day while the light itself was the result of God's first day of creation. The celestial lights are nothing more than concentrations of the light in circumscribed areas. In each instance, they are only reflective of the divine light which is the immanent God of all.

In view of this clear-cut observation it is not hard to conceive of a world in which the sun, moon, and stars have been removed without resulting in darkness! Writing in his first epistle, John says, ". . . God is light and in him is no darkness at all" (1 John 1:5). Malachi promised that the day would come when "[shall] the sun of righteousness rise with healing in his wings" (Malachi 4:2). And when Jesus, the Son of God who is the source of all light, came into the world, He declared, "I am the light of the world" (John 8:12; 9:5). Now the Apocalypse informs us that "the city has no need of the sun or moon to shine upon it, for the glory of God is its light, and its lamp is the Lamb" (Revelation 21:23; cf. 22:5 RSV). We are further told that those who surround the throne, having come out of great tribulation, shall dwell where "the sun shall not strike them, nor any scorching heat" (7:16 RSV). The Trinity, source of ineffable light, will provide all the light needed in the heavenly state.

Of additonal insight is the story of Jesus' transfiguration where ". . . his face shone like the sun, and his garments became white as light" (Matthew 17:2 RSV). This was a foretaste of what we may anticipate in the world to come. In the center of the vision given to John stood one whose "face was like the sun shining in full strength" (Revelation 1:16; cf. 10:1 RSV). It was this same light which struck Saul of Tarsus with temporary blindness (Acts 9:3, 8, 9) and was later described by him as ". . . a light from heaven, brighter than the sun, shining round me . . ." (Acts 26:13 RSV). Thus we perceive that no luminous bodies will be needed to reflect the light of God where He is so fully present. The only possible reflection of divine brightness in heaven will be the people themselves whom Jesus says "will shine like the sun in the kingdom of their Father . . ." (Matthew 13:43 RSV).

Renovation of the Urban Center

Talk about urban renewal! If the transformation brought to metropolitan slum areas by man's skill at modernizing his environment is thought to be a spectacular achievement, what must the righteous have yet to see in the new Jerusalem! On earth, crews of workmen set themselves to the task of clearing away the downtown eyesores and replacing them with high-rise offices. In the process, vermin-infested tenements are obliterated and the cesspools of disease and pollution are done away. God must have something of the same thing in mind in the plans for the New Jerusalem, plans which are shared with us in the Book of Revelation. "But nothing unclean shall enter it, nor anyone who practices abomination or falsehood, but only those who are written in the Lamb's book of life" (Revelation 21:27 RSV) and "there shall no more be anything accursed . . ." (22:3 RSV).

In the initial section of this chapter we looked at the pure river flowing from the midst of this city. Beside that river there is to be ". . . the tree of life with its twelve kinds of fruit, yielding its fruit each month; and the leaves of the tree were for the healing of the nations" (22:2 RSV). Obviously, the fruit of this tree, whose roots draw from the pure water of life in the river, are health-giving like that which grew on the tree of life in the Garden of Eden (Genesis 2:9). The fruit on that tree would have made man live forever, but Adam chose instead to eat from the forbidden tree of the knowledge of good and evil. For that sin he was driven from the garden and debarred from the tree of life (Genesis 3:22–24). Someday, in the heavenly world, God's redeemed children will be permitted access to that old life-giving tree and we shall live forever!

The account states that the renovated city of God was seen "coming down . . . out of heaven prepared as a bride adorned for her husband" (Revelation 21:2). The New Jerusalem is to be understood, therefore, as both a city and a people. It is likely that this city will be suspended in the air above the land of Palestine during the Millennium and, at its end, will descend to the renewed earth. Another reference is made to the Bride as the holy city in verse nine of this same chapter. Since the Bride is always to be equated in Scripture with the Church, it is likely that this is where the translated Church of Christ will dwell during the millennial reign. This explains how glorified bodies (in the exalted city above the earth) and mortal bodies (on the earth) can live together for the thousand years of peace. The city is seen as something "coming down," however, which means that its final position will be on the earth. This will take place after the burning holocaust which purifies the world at the genesis of the coming eternal state. While the city is suspended above the earth, the saints who have had part in the first resurrection will probably share with the Bride. This seems to be borne out by John's seeing twelve gates inscribed with the names of the Jewish tribes and twelve foundation stones inscribed with the names of the apostles.

Can we begin to conceive the breathtaking beauty of a city which has streets of transparent gold and whose walls are everywhere plastered with precious gems? With the light of God sparkling on each jeweled prism and producing a kaleidoscope of brilliant light, heaven must be fantastic beyond our loftiest expectation. "By its light shall the nations [peoples] walk . . ." (Revelation 21:24 RSV). And no wonder! From this city, which will be the center of the heavenly world, the glorified sons of God will have access to all the earth and the farthest reaches of the spaceless universe. Jesus may have had this in mind when He said, "In my Father's house are many rooms . . ." (John 14:2 RSV). Indeed, the Father's house is vaster by far than our telescopes suggest.

God's New People

"Behold, the dwelling of God is with men. He will dwell with them and they shall be his people, and God Himself will be with them" (Revelation 21:3 RSV). From the beginning of man's existence, the Lord God has been creating a people for Himself. After all the centuries and millennia of discipline, chastisement, and punishment—at last, His plan will be completed. The relationship will be what man has dreamed about and sought after through all his days: "I will be his God and he shall be my son" (21:7). That is the divine promise to him who overcomes in the struggle against evil. Of course, the victory itself belongs to Christ whose Spirit wins for him who trusts in His atoning work on the cross.

To worship and glorify God who has redeemed us will fill our days with joy and gladness. We "shall see his face, and his name shall be on [our] foreheads" (22:4 RSV). Oh, the joy of seeing Him whom our hearts have felt and our minds have followed! Man's deepest desire is to *see* God. To look upon the face of His redeeming Son who has saved us from death and hell will be to know the satisfaction of our eternal aspirations.

No more will the wicked shatter the blessedness of His people. No more will Satan interfere. No more will man struggle against the curses of our modern world—scourges like war, pollution, and starvation. ". . . as for the cowardly, the faithless, the polluted, as for murderers, fornicators, sorcerers, idolaters, and all liars, their lot shall be in the lake that burns with fire and brimstone . . ." (21:8 RSV). Emphasizing the same point of exclusion of everyone and everything which would contaminate the new world, John says, "Outside the city are those who have strayed away from God, and the sorcerers, and the immoral and murderers, and idolaters, and all who love to lie, and do so" (22:15 LB). Emphatically, the impression given by the prophecy of John is that the heavenly world will be "a prepared place for a prepared people"!

Characteristics of the Life to Come

No one will die in heaven. "The last enemy that shall be destroyed is death" (1 Corinthians 15:26). And in that life for which all creation groans ". . . death shall be no more" (21:4 RSV). The child of God will be immortal in his glorified body, a body like unto that of Jesus following the Resurrection. The entire verse from which the above quote is taken includes more than death in its list of missing things.

> He will wipe away every tear from their eyes, and death shall be
> no more, neither shall there be mourning nor crying nor pain
> anymore, for the former things have passed away.
>
> v. 24 RSV

These words clarify more than at first meets the eye. If there are no tears or pain, then everything which has caused man trouble in his earthly pilgrimage will be missing. This does not imply stagnation in a sterile climate. Far from it. What it does imply is that the righteous will finally be able to be and do that which God originally intended for them. There will be no deterrents to hinder his growth and loving service. The hindrances will have been conquered and rendered impotent as we pass through the gates of the city.

Contrary to the scholarly opinions of many within the Church today, God has chosen to reveal a great part of His plan for the world. The future is not shrouded in mystery for him who will arduously search the Scriptures. The Bible—both Old and New Testaments—is God's message to man. For too long we have either ignored it or mutilated it with our irreverent criticisms. It is time that we allow the Scriptures to speak to us in their clear, powerful, divine voice. Any man can understand enough prophecy not to be caught by surprise when the Lord comes for His Church. The world events which are taking place all around us in these days are all a part of the divine plan. We are foolish beyond words to describe if we neglect the prophetic calendar and guidebook which can lead us out of a world destined for judgment.

While God has chosen to reveal much of His plan for the winding up of the present world order, He has told us very little about the eternal dimension which we have been discussing in this chapter. That is His secret which He is keeping as a surprise for His own. What little we have been permitted to see has only whetted our appetites for more. Therefore, we have begun the journey to "Canaan's fair and happy land" and some of us are well on our way. The farther along the way we get, the more excited we become. But let us be patient, "Looking for that blessed hope . . ." (Titus 2:13) until the promise of God is fulfilled in us on the hills of that eternal city!

13
Why Believe the Time Is Now?

A Perspective on History

Zephaniah warned the Israelites in the seventh century before Christ that the Chaldeans were coming. No one would believe it. But they came anyway and the people were carried into captivity. Jesus warned the Jews that their nation would be overrun and the Temple destroyed within a generation. Nobody believed it. But the Romans came and the last vestige of a nation destined to be God's light to the world was erased from the scene. The United States has been the world's leading power for a century. Voices are now warning that the end of our glory is drawing near, that "the great democracy" is about to end. But does anyone believe it? Only a scattered handful. Before the day of America's grandeur it was England who stood on the top of the world. And prior to England it was France, Spain, Rome, Greece, Egypt, and Babylon. Every time there were seers to predict what was soon to happen, but in no case did enough people believe it to alter the destiny of an empire.

In *The Decline and Fall of the Roman Empire,* Gibbon gives several reasons for the deterioration and collapse of Rome. The people played loose with morals to the point of desecrating the family and nearly destroying the home. When the family goes, the nation goes, too. Taxes were exorbitant and unwisely used to provide support and entertainment for the masses, many of whom did not contribute their share. Practically all the populace was obsessed with an insatiable thirst for pleasure. Sports were more important than employment or faith. And the sports became more and more sadistic and brutal. A massive system of weaponry was created and continuously added to under the certainty of a false security. All the while there was an inner decay at the heart of the empire—a rejection of responsiblity on the part of the citizens them-selves. What was probably worst of all, religion—pagan as it may have been—was neglected and materialism smothered almost every trace of awe and reverence for the supernatural.

History reveals that, while some empires have gone down in battle and others have been taken without a shot, the general pattern has been the same. One of the above criteria always characterizes a fallen people. Usually there is a combination of several or all of them. Anyone can easily see that the United States fits the total description to perfection. But the most telling observation of our modern time is that, for the first time, one or more of these characteristics can be found in *every* nation on the face of the earth. In fact, the whole world in general is accurately pictured in Gibbon's five points of decline in the Roman Empire. This, in itself, is one good reason to believe, from a historical analysis alone, that the human race as a whole is nearing its demise.

Widespread Interest in Prophecy

Every generation has a few persons concerned enough with prophecy to speak out on the subject. Occasionally, some enthusiastic seer will try to pinpoint the exact date of the end of the world. Not since the days of the New Testament Church, however, has there been as much worldwide interest in biblical prophecy as in the last ten years. Quite suddenly, the Holy Spirit seems to be removing the scales from our eyes and people everywhere, especially young people, are asking for illumina-tion on the subject of "last things." Even people who have not been too involved in the religious activity of their home church are beginning to get excited about the prospects for the consummation of the ages inher-ent in our time. When Michael the Archangel concluded his instruc-tions to Daniel relating to the end of the world, he specifically described our own age as the time when the prophecies would be understood.

> "But Daniel, keep this prophecy a secret; seal it up so that it will not be understood until the end times, when travel and education shall be vastly increased!"
>
> Daniel 12:4 LB

Young people have become strangely knowledgeable in biblical prophecy. It has happened almost spontaneously and with very little instruction. It is as if the Spirit had broken open His sealed mysteries and poured them into the hearts and minds of millions of youthful witnesses. Scientists, educators, philosophers, business men, professional people, and housewives are sharing the prophetic word. Once in a while a clergyman is found who will risk a few words on the subject! Back in the seventeenth century, Isaac Newton said, "About the Time of the End, a body of men will be raised up who will turn to the Prophecies, and insist upon their literal interpretations, in the midst of much clamor and opposition." That time is now. The prophets are crying out, "Thus saith the Lord!" and the institutional Church and some of its supported seminaries are providing the opposition. Daniel's heavenly visitor had a sobering word to say about this rebel attitude.

"Go now, Daniel, for what I have said is not to be understood until the time of the end. Many shall be purified by great trials and persecutions. But the wicked shall continue in their wickedness, and none of them will understand. Only those who are willing to learn will know what it means."

Daniel 12:9, 10 LB

Considering the incontestable evidence that every prophecy relating to the birth of Christ, the first Advent of the Messiah, was fulfilled to the letter, it would be a bit unexplainable if we were to doubt the certainty of literal fulfillment for those having to do with His return. And it would also be strange for disciples of Christ to question the integrity of Jesus or the veracity of His words about the kind of conditions which will prevail on the earth immediately before His Second Advent. He has never been found wrong. Lately, many of His prophetic words are coming true in precise detail as He said they would.

Scarcely any generation since the days of Christ has been without some signs of the end. Only in the last three decades have we seen so many prophecies being brought to pass all at once. *This makes our time different from all previous periods in history.* Those who argue that there have always been signs and prophets to call attention to them do not seriously consider the rapid multiplication of those signs in our day. To fail to make that vitally significant observation is tragic.

International Preparation for the End

When a man has a premonition that he is going to die, he almost always acts in a certain way. His demeanor will become deeply serious and, with the strength and time he has left, a man inevitably tries to get his affairs in shape and his house in order. We are seeing exactly this kind of serious concentration and hurried effort by the nations today. There is a growing premonition that civilization is in its last hours. And instead of turning to God in faith and relaxing in His divine providence, we intensify our human drive to set straight the house of the world. A kind of death struggle is upon the nations as a rebel race gives one last push to building a perfect kingdom of man. At the bottom of our frantic struggle is an international awareness that we have dug our own grave and that the shroud is laid out.

Everything on the world scene is shaping up just as the Bible says it will at the end. Man is doing what is natural in the approach of global death. God has told us that certain things will happen as the world's breath grows short. In a quick recap of what has been said in foregoing pages, let us look at some of the most obvious signs of the end of the age as the Word of God portrays it.

We have seen the restoration of the Jewish people in their own land by act of the United Nations. The one unfulfilled prophecy, which annulled all talk of the coming of Christ and the winding up of our world order in the past, was the promise of Israel's return to Palestine. That had to take place before the end could come. And it did happen in 1948. Furthermore, the Jews were promised control of the holy city again. For the first time since the days of Christ the city of Jerusalem was recaptured in 1967. Our generation has seen history made and prophecy realized in an astounding manner. Jesus clearly affirmed that the Jews would be in Palestine and Jerusalem when He returns. He also stated that "this generation [the generation living when the Jewish nation is restored] will not pass away till all these things take place" (Matthew 24:34; Mark 13:30; Luke 21:32). The generation which has seen these things transpire is ours!

Scripture indicates that the Temple of the Jews will be rebuilt on Mount Zion before the *parousia* (2 Thessalonians 2; Matthew 24:15, 16). As yet that Temple is not constructed, but plans are underway to erect the edifice soon. Since such a feat could be on its way within a matter of months, and since the Church will be translated before its construction by Antichrist, the coming of Christ for His Bride could happen tonight!

Ezekiel is not at all cryptic when he tells us that Russia and her confederates will invade Israel. Nor are we left in the dark as to what to expect from the Arabic world including both the African Arabs (Libya) and the Black Africans (Ethiopia). The relationship between Russia and the Arabs today is exactly what we should expect if the end is near. And the mighty hosts of China, now in readiness to cross the Euphrates River and share in the final war, is an integral part of the picture. No one can possibly miss the significance of the Common Market in Europe which has laid the groundwork out of which the revived Roman Empire shall rise and from which will issue the Antichrist.

All over the world the cry is raised, "Peace! Peace!" Young men burn their draft cards or seek asylum in other countries rather than accept the draft. The Church has joined in the religious-sounding demands for a world without war. Masses of people display the crow's foot as their expression of resistance to war. Nevertheless, in the midst of all the talk about world peace the nations continue to badger one another and prepare for the war of all wars which everyone subconsciously knows to be on the way. Never before have men been more interested in peace and less able to achieve it than right now!

Added to this should be a word about mankind's rabid interest in the heavens. Jesus said that there would be signs in the sun and other heavenly bodies. While His specific reference was to the change that will take place in these luminaries themselves, it is of importance to note that man is more interested in the moon and surrounding planets today than ever before. Our space program grows out of an insatiable desire to know more about the distant bodies of light in the heavens. And in conjunction with this scientific probe is the revival of pagan star-worship by millions of duped people who live on the authority of astrological prognosticators. Our obsession with the sun, moon, and stars keeps us looking up. That may be a form of preparation for our seeing the upheaval in the heavens and the appearing of Christ in the clouds of judgment!

Everybody Knows the Trouble We've Seen

Famine stalks the earth and reaps untold numbers of men, women, and children. Lean, gaunt bodies with huge eyes staring out at us in helplessness greet us in the daily newspapers and on television. Earthquakes occur lately with more frequency and do more damage in life and property than ever before. Seismologists are predicting that the problem is getting worse, that we are sitting on a keg of dynamite which can be ignited at any moment. Violence in the streets has become an international concern. Not too long ago, campuses were in disarray, conventions were invaded, ghettos were burned, and people are still afraid to walk the streets alone in our major cities. Racial tension is at an all-time high even though blacks and whites keep smiling as though the whole thing were under control. Authority in government, education, religion, and the home is rejected. Every individual does as he pleases and the whole world suffers. The "bewilderment" of which the Lord spoke (Luke 21:25) is all around us.

These are the times when men "bring upon themselves quick destruction" (2 Peter 2:1). An example of this is found in what was experienced by the people of Hiroshima and has been feared by every man alive since that sad day. But we have many ways of bringing quick death to ourselves and others. Our drug epidemic is leaving tragedy in its wake. Wild and senseless abandonment to sex and perversion is only symptomatic of our bent toward self-destruction. Experimentation with evil powers, demonic forces, astrology, and satanic cultism brings with it insanity and uncontrollable fear.

Religious institutions are dying everywhere. The organized Church is in serious trouble, so much so that large groups have decided to pool their dwindling forces in a united conglomerate. Maybe the image of bigness and oneness and cooperation will give them a few more days of grace. All of it is being promoted under the ruse of becoming the Church of Christ in unity of purpose and spirit. Regardless as to what we hear in glowing pronouncements of positive value in the movement, what we see does not bear out the truth of the praises sounded by the uniting strategists. The faith of the apostles is so emasculated of its content and power that there is nothing left but a religious shell. If the living gospel of Jesus Christ were to be put in that brittle shell it would literally explode! No one pays much attention anymore to the organized Church, its theological schools, or its official declarations. Why should he? There is nothing really distinctive about the Church today except in rare instances where a local congregation has been "turned on" by the Holy Spirit. This desiccated shell of uniting organizations has served the cause of Satan well in paving the way for the apostate institutions of the tribulation and its false prophet.

One Encouraging Word

Right in the middle of the wickedness, pride, and apostasy of these days the Holy Spirit is doing a great work. The laity is bypassing the normal busyness of the Church and discovering the power of a Spirit-filled life. Thousands of lay people from nearly all denominations including the Roman Catholic fellowship are teaming up in mission outside the walls of their own parish. Several campus organizations have sprung up to witness to college students. Prayer groups of teen-agers are forming in high schools. In-depth Bible study cells are being arranged by hungry men and women who have not been fed from the Word in their local churches. And the most amazing thing of all is that millions of young people, many of whom had been on dope and sex, have joined the Jesus Movement. These youth are radiant in their faith and absolutely unafraid to speak out for Jesus to anyone they meet. Something contagious lingers about their presence and it is hard to be critical of them or their methods without feeling guilty. The transformation in their style of life and the *Shekinah* (presence of God) on their countenances are two evidences of the work of the Lord which cannot be missed.

The name of Jesus is being seen everywhere as though it belongs in all areas of man's culture. And, indeed, it does. Certainly, there is a chance that His worthy name may be prostituted in some instances by being associated with evil surroundings. But He who was unafraid of being contaminated by associating with sinners is not at all alarmed in finding His name in strange and even wicked places. Where else would we expect to find Him if He were here in the flesh?

The whole world is having a phenomenal opportunity to become acquainted with Jesus Christ. No one can plead ignorance any longer. Christ is all about us without disguise. His Holy Spirit is working in the open and lives are being touched in every city and hamlet of the world. Mass communication media are getting involved in the work of the Lord —often without knowing it! The entire spiritual aura prevailing in our world of sham and pretense is a sure sign that God is "pouring out His Spirit upon all flesh" *(see* Joel 2:28 and Acts 2:17).

As this Spirit confronts the world not every person will be saved. There is no warrant in the Scriptures for believing that such will ever happen. Some are being redeemed and made a part of that Bride for whom our Lord is soon to come. But multitudes are becoming adamant against this "new thing" which the Lord is doing and they are resisting the Spirit. Often these people are staid members of the institutional Church and regular attenders at its services of worship. Believers are becoming bolder to witness and a polarization is developing that will divide the world into two distinct camps—the Bride and the rejected.

Jesus said, "I came to cast fire on the earth . . . Do you think that I have come to give peace . . . ? No, I tell you, but rather division" (Luke 12:49, 51 RSV). By that our Lord acknowledged that His purpose in the world now is polarization since there can be no peace for anyone when Christ is not taken seriously. When men experience the fire of God there will be both an honoring of their witness and a persecution of themselves. We should expect a time of persecution soon in which Christian witnesses will become Christian martyrs.

While the Spirit of God is moving in the world and many are coming to know Christ, there is little reason to believe that we are on the verge of a great revival. Our Saviour suggested that He might find a scarcity of faith on the earth when He returns (Luke 18:8). The description which He gives of the end-times as being like the days of Noah would not imply a great revival. Paul reminds us that we should not let ourselves be deceived because the Day of the Lord will not come "except there come a falling away first" (2 Thessalonians 2:3). Many who are coming to new life in the Spirit are men and women who had given up on the institutional Church. And, by the same token, many who are falling away from the Lord are those within the ecclesiastical organization who are too proud of their Pharisaism to bow before the Saviour.

These are great and terrible days to be alive. They are both exciting and fearful—exciting because the Lord is due to come at any moment —fearful because so many are not ready to enter in with Him to the Marriage Supper of the Lamb. To the people who continue to ignore the mighty penetration of the Spirit in these latter days, we must carry the dual message of impending judgment or joyous deliverance. To those who are watching for His appearing, we must offer words of encouragement and assurance. And to Him who will one day rend the eastern sky with a shout, we must say,

"Come, Lord Jesus!"

Bibliography

Barnhouse, Donald G. *Revelation: An Expositional Commentary.* Grand Rapids: Zondervan Publishing House, 1971.

Beasley-Murray, George R. *Highlights of the Book of Revelation.* Nashville: Broadman Press, 1971.

Berkouwer, Gerrit C. *The Return of Christ,* vol. 12. Grand Rapids: Wm. B. Eerdmans Publishing Co., 1952.

Bierdewolf, William E. *The Second Coming Bible.* Grand Rapids: Baker Book House, 1972.

Blackstone, W. E. *Jesus Is Coming.* New York: Fleming H. Revell Company, 1932.

Bloomfield, Arthur E. *All Things New.* Minneapolis: Bethany Fellowship, Inc. 1959.

————. *Signs of His Coming.* Minneapolis: Bethany Fellowship, Inc., 1962.

————. *The End of the Days.* Minneapolis: Bethany Fellowship, Inc., 1961.

————. *A Survey of Bible Prophecy.* Minneapolis: Bethany Fellowship, Inc., 1971.

Buxton, Clyne W. *Expect These Things.* Old Tappan: Fleming H. Revell Company, 1973.

Criswell, W. A. *Expository Sermons on Revelation:* Five Volumes Complete and Unabridged in One. Grand Rapids: Zondervan Publishing House, 1961–66.

DeHaan, Martin R. *The Second Coming of Jesus.* Grand Rapids: Zondervan Publishing House, 1944.

DeHaan, Richard W. *Israel and the Nations in Prophecy.* Grand Rapids: Zondervan Publishing House, 1971.

Duty, Guy. *Christ's Coming and the World Church.* Minneapolis: Bethany Fellowship, Inc., 1971.

Eade, Arthur T. *The Second Coming of Christ: The New Panorama Bible Study Course #3.* Westwood: Fleming H. Revell Company, 1966.

Ehrlich, Paul R. *The Population Bomb.* New York: Ballantine Books, 1968.

Ehrlich, Paul R. and Anne H. *Population, Resources, Environment.* San Francisco: W. H. Freeman Co., 1970.

Feinberg, Charles Lee, ed. *Prophecy and the Seventies.* Chicago: Moody Press, 1971.

————. *Focus on Prophecy.* Westwood: Fleming H. Revell Company, 1964.

Guy, H. A. *The New Testament Doctrine of 'Last Things'.* London: Oxford Press, 1948.

Hamilton, Michael. *This Little Planet.* New York: Chas. Scribner's Sons, 1971.

Hanson, Richard S. *The Future of the Great Planet Earth.* Minneapolis: Augsburg Publishing House, 1972.

Harrison, William K. *Hope Triumphant.* Chicago: Moody Press, 1966.

Henry, Carl F. H., ed. *Prophecy in the Making.* Carol Stream, Ill.: Creation House, 1971.

Hoyt, Herman A. *The End Times.* Chicago: Moody Press, 1969.

Imsland, Donald. *Celebrate the Earth.* Minneapolis: Augsburg Publishing House, 1971.

Kirban, Salem. *Guide to Survival*. Wheaton, Ill.: Tyndale House Publishers, 1968

————. *666*. Wheaton, Ill.: Tyndale House Publishers, 1970.

————. *I Predict*. Huntington Valley, Pa.: Salem Kirban, Inc., n.d.

Koch, Kurt. *Day X*. Grand Rapids: Kregel Publications, 1969.

Ladd, George Eldon. *A Commentary on the Revelation of John*. Grand Rapids: Wm. B. Eerdmans Publishing Co., 1971.

LaHaye, Tim. *The Beginning of the End*. Wheaton, Ill.: Tyndale House Publishers, 1972.

Lindsey, Hal and Carlson, C. C. *The Late Great Planet Earth*. Grand Rapids: Zondervan Publishing House, 1970.

Logsdon, S. Franklin. *Profiles of Prophecy*. Grand Rapids: Zondervan Publishing House, 1969.

Mackintosh, C. H. *The Lord's Coming*. Chicago: Moody Press, n.d.

Mauro, Philip. *Of Things Which Soon Must Come to Pass*. Swengel, Pa.: Reiner Publications, 1971.

McKee, Bill. *Orbit of Ashes*. Wheaton, Ill.: Tyndale House Publishers, 1972.

McMillen. S. I. *Discern These Times*. Old Tappan, N.J.: Fleming H. Revell Company, 1971.

Pache, Rene. *The Return of Jesus Christ*. Chicago: Moody Press, 1955.

Pentecost, J. Dwight. *Things to Come*. Grand Rapids: Zondervan Publishing House, 1958.

Santmire, H. Paul. *Brother Earth*. Camden, N.J.: Thomas Nelson Inc., 1970.

Schaeffer, Francis. *Pollution and the Death of Man*. Wheaton, Ill.: Tyndale House Publishers, 1970.

Scott, Walter. *Exposition on the Revelation of Jesus Christ*. Westwood, N.J.: Fleming H. Revell Company, n.d.

Seiss, J. A. *The Apocalypse*. Grand Rapids: Zondervan Publishing House, n.d.

Smith, Wilbur. *The Biblical Doctrine of Heaven*. Chicago: Moody Press, 1968.

————. *You Can Know the Future*. Glendale, Calif.: Regal Books, 1971.

Stedman, Ray C. *What on Earth's Going to Happen?* Glendale, Calif.: Regal Books, 1970.

Strauss, Lehman. *The End of This Present World*. Grand Rapids: Zondervan Publishing House, 1968.

Taylor, Gordan Rattray. *The Doomsday Book*. New York: World Publishing Company, 1971.

Walvoord, John F. *Daniel*. Chicago: Moody Press, 1970.

————. *The Revelation of Jesus Christ*. Chicago: Moody Press, 1966.

————. *Israel in Prophecy*. Grand Rapids: Zondervan Publishing House, 1962.

————. *The Return of the Lord*. Grand Rapids: Zondervan Publishing House (Dunham), 1955.

White, John Wesley. *Re-entry*. Grand Rapids: Zondervan Publishing House, 1970.

Wilkerson, David, ed. *Jesus Christ: Solid Rock*. Grand Rapids: Zondervan Publishing House, 1972.

Willis, Charles D. *End of Days: 1971–2001*. Jericho, N.Y.: Exposition Press, Inc., 1972.

Wood, A. S. *Signs of the Times*. Grand Rapids: Baker Book House, 1971.

Wood, Leon. *A Commentary on Daniel*. Grand Rapids: Zondervan Publishing House, 1972.

Woodson, Leslie. *Hell and Salvation*. Old Tappan, N.J.: Fleming H. Revell Company, 1973.